Introduction

The participating U.S. Department of Defense (DoD) and Federal oversight agencies, which comprise the Southwest Asia Joint Planning Group, are pleased to present the Fiscal Year 2014 Comprehensive Oversight Plan for Southwest Asia (FY 2014 COPSWA). This annual plan reflects essential interagency collaboration within the oversight community to provide comprehensive reviews of contingency expenditures, to identify whether critical oversight gaps exist, and to recommend actions to address those gaps.

The FY 2014 COPSWA incorporates the planned and ongoing oversight by the Inspectors General of the DoD (DoD OIG), U.S. Department of State (DOS OIG), and the U.S. Agency for International Development (USAID OIG); the Special Inspector General for Afghanistan Reconstruction (SIGAR); the U.S. Army Audit Agency (AAA); the Naval Audit Service (NAVAUDSVC); and the U.S. Air Force Audit Agency (AFAA). The FY 2014 update also includes ongoing oversight efforts by the U.S. Government Accountability Office (GAO) related to Southwest Asia. This oversight plan is as of September 1, 2013.

In March 2013, the Special Inspector General for Iraq Reconstruction (SIGIR) culminated its nine-year mission in the issuance of its study, "Learning From Iraq: A Final Report From the Special Inspector General for Iraq Reconstruction." As such, SIGIR did not submit carryover or new oversight projects for the FY 2014 COPSWA. For a listing of products that were completed during FY 2013 for each agency, see Section 4.2.

Although the COPSWA does not report law enforcement efforts and outcomes, it is important to note that when criminal activity is suspected during the course of an audit, evaluation, or inspection, the allegations are referred to the respective law enforcement component. Specifically, these components are the Defense Criminal Investigative Service, which is the law enforcement arm of the DoD OIG; the SIGAR and SIGIR Investigations Directorates; the Offices of Investigations for the DOS OIG and the USAID OIG; the U.S. Army Criminal Investigative Command, Major Procurement Fraud Unit; the Air Force Office of Special Investigations; and the Naval Criminal Investigative Service. Each of these agencies is a member of the International Contract Corruption Task Force, which combines agency resources to collectively and efficiently deconflict and investigate public corruption and contract fraud in Southwest Asia.

As emphasis continues on the U.S. military, diplomatic, and development missions in Afghanistan, the COPSWA includes an updated FY 2014 Joint Strategic Oversight Plan for Afghanistan, located at Section 1.0. This plan reflects the oversight of activities related to the transition from a military-led to a civilian-led U.S. mission in Afghanistan. The withdrawal of U.S. forces and base closures may impede the ability of the oversight agencies and contracting officer representatives to visit project field sites to conduct oversight of service and construction contracts and to monitor the progress of transition and sustainment activities. However, through the end of 2014, oversight efforts will continue, consistent with the security posture of U.S. forces and the Command's ability to provide support.

In the interest of logical clarity and to better fit with the concerns of the transfer of greater security and other responsibilities to the Government of the Islamic Republic of Afghanistan (GIRoA), the Joint Strategic Oversight Plan for Afghanistan was updated from 22 strategic issue areas in FY 2013 to 11 strategic issue areas for FY 2014. These issues are presented in two sections: Reconstruction (7 issues), and Other Than Reconstruction (4 issues). Specific oversight projects that address these issues are identified in Section 1.2 of the FY 2014 COPSWA. Each project identifies the strategic issue(s) that are being addressed. Referring to the strategic issue identified in the Joint Strategic Oversight Plan for Afghanistan will describe the strategic importance of why the individual oversight projects were selected for execution in FY 2014.

The COPSWA includes descriptions of oversight projects that directly affect efforts in Southwest Asia and surrounding areas. The projects may be conducted exclusively in theater, require travel into theater, or be conducted outside the theater, such as solely in the continental United States (CONUS). The FY 2014 COPSWA edition is organized in Sections (1.2) Afghanistan only—by oversight agency; (1.3) Afghanistan only—by strategic oversight issue; and (2) Other than Afghanistan. In Section 1, the strategic issue(s) is identified for each project. In Section 2, the impacted country(s) is identified for each project, including Iraq, Kuwait, Kyrgyzstan, Pakistan, and other Southwest Asia countries. The full list of strategic issues and countries can be found on page iv. Each COPSWA section groups projects by the executing oversight agency. The individual oversight projects are listed in the order of the COPSWA reference number, which is a unique identifier assigned for tracking purposes only.

Our agencies continue to work together through the Southwest Asia Joint Planning Group to coordinate and provide effective oversight of the U.S.-led efforts in Southwest Asia. We also continue to coordinate oversight plans through improved communications among the members on a regular basis and on individual projects as they are proposed throughout the year. We will update this plan in September 2014.

REQUIRED OVERSIGHT. The COPSWA was first issued in June 2008 (and each year since) in accordance with the requirements of Public Law 110-181, "The National Defense Authorization Act for Fiscal Year 2008," section 842, "Investigation of Waste, Fraud, and Abuse in Wartime Contracts and Contracting Processes in Iraq and Afghanistan," January 28, 2008. In 2009, we began to include additional oversight requirements as directed by Public Law 110-417, "The National Defense Authorization Act for Fiscal Year 2009," section 852, "Comprehensive Audit of Spare Parts, Purchases, and Depot Overhaul and Maintenance of Equipment For Operations in Iraq and Afghanistan," October 14, 2008 (for reporting purposes, see Section 3). Additional information on Sections 842 and 852, respectively, can be found in Appendix B.

EXPANSION OF THE OVERSIGHT PLAN TO INCLUDE ADDITIONAL AREAS SUPPORTING THE U.S. MISSION IN SOUTHWEST ASIA. We expanded this oversight plan beyond the statutory mandate to show the audit, inspection, and evaluation work identified for Afghanistan and the rest of the U.S. Central Command's area of responsibility, which is comprised of a total of 20 countries. For a listing of these countries, see page iv.

Summary of FY 2014 Oversight Activities

TABLE 1. FY 2014 ONGOING AND PLANNED OVERSIGHT PROJECTS
BY ORGANIZATION

ORGANIZATION	ONGOING	PLANNED
DoD OIG	25	16
AAA	11	1
NAVAUDSVC	4	0
AFAA	5	7
SIGAR	63	22
DOS OIG	8	16
USAID OIG	55	68
GAO	14	0
Total Projects = 315	185	130

TABLE 2. FY 2014 ONGOING AND PLANNED OVERSIGHT PROJECTS
IMPACTING AFGHANISTAN, OTHER SOUTHWEST ASIA COUNTRIES, AND
CONUS

ORGANIZATION	AFGHANISTAN	OTHER SOUTHWEST ASIA COUNTRIES
DoD OIG	27	22
AAA	10	3
NAVAUDSVC	2	5
AFAA	11	28
SIGAR	85	0
DOS OIG	9	15
USAID OIG	93	30
GAO	12	3

Note: One project may impact two or more countries.

TABLE 3. FY 2014 STRATEGIC OVERSIGHT ISSUES FOR AFGHANISTAN

Section 1. Reconstruction
1. Building the Capacity and Capabilities of the Afghan National Security Forces and Administering and Maintaining Accountability of the Afghanistan Security Forces Fund
2. Building Afghan Governance Capacity
3. Sustaining U.S. Investment in Afghan Institutions and Infrastructure
4. Executing and Sustaining Counternarcotics Programs
5. Implementing Anti-Corruption Initiatives
6. Planning, Coordinating, and Providing Stewardship of Direct and Indirect Assistance Funds and Programs
7. Awarding and Administering Reconstruction Contracts
Section 2. Other Than Reconstruction
8. Health and Safety
9. Retrograde and Property Management
10. Contract Management and Oversight
11. Transition Planning and Execution

TABLE 4. SOUTHWEST ASIA COUNTRY CODES
(U.S. CENTRAL COMMAND'S AREA OF RESPONSIBILITY)

AF	Afghanistan	OM	Oman
BH	Bahrain	PK	Pakistan
EG	Egypt	QA	Qatar
IR	Iran, Islamic Republic of	SA	Saudi Arabia
IQ	Iraq	SY	Syrian Arab Republic
JO	Jordan	TJ	Tajikistan
KZ	Kazakhstan	TM	Turkmenistan
KW	Kuwait	AE	United Arab Emirates
KG	Kyrgyzstan	UZ	Uzbekistan
LB	Lebanon	YE	Yemen
Southwest Asia issue with work conducted elsewhere:			
CONUS = Continental United States OCONUS = Outside the Continental U.S.		Other/Multiple = Not exclusively a Southwest Asia country.	

Source: International Organization for Standardization, ISO 3166-1-Alpha-2 Country Codes.

Contents

Department of Defense Office of Inspector General
U.S. Army Audit Agency
Naval Audit Service
U.S. Air Force Audit Agency
Special Inspector General for Afghanistan Reconstruction
Department of State Office of Inspector General
U.S. Agency for International Development Office of Inspector General
U.S. Government Accountability Office

1. Building the Capacity and Capabilities of the ANSF and Administering and Maintaining Accountability of the ASFF
2. Building Afghan Governance Capacity
3. Sustaining U.S. Investment in Afghan Institutions and Infrastructure
4. Executing and Sustaining Counternarcotics Programs
5. Implementing Anti-Corruption Initiatives
6. Planning, Coordinating, and Providing Stewardship of Direct and Indirect Assistance Funds and Programs
7. Awarding and Administering Reconstruction Contracts
8. Health and Safety
9. Retrograde and Property Management
10. Contract Management and Oversight
11. Transition Planning and Execution

Department of Defense Office of Inspector General
U.S. Army Audit Agency
Naval Audit Service
U.S. Air Force Audit Agency
Department of State Office of Inspector General
U.S. Agency for International Development Office of Inspector General
U.S. Government Accountability Office

Contents (cont'd)

Section 1. Afghanistan Projects

Section 1.0. FY 2014 Joint Strategic Oversight Plan for Afghanistan

INTRODUCTION

On June 18, 2013, NATO Secretary General Anders Fogh Rasmussen welcomed the announcement by President Hamid Karzai of Afghanistan of the fifth and final group of Afghan provinces, cities and districts to undergo transition. This decision marked an important milestone, when the Afghan security forces--Afghan soldiers and police--would take the lead for the country's security. At the same time, International Security Assistance Force (ISAF) forces were shifting from a combat to a support role.

On June 14, 2013, the White House released the "Letter from the President–Regarding the War Powers Resolution." In the letter, President Barack Obama reports:

> United States Armed Forces continue to pursue and engage remaining al-Qa'ida and Taliban fighters in Afghanistan while transitioning to an Afghan security lead. The Afghanistan Force Management Level is approximately 62,000 U.S. forces. Approximately 49,000 of these forces are assigned to the North Atlantic Treaty Organization (NATO)-led International Security Assistance Force (ISAF) in Afghanistan. Further Presidentially directed force reductions will continue to the 34,000 level by February 12, 2014. Fifty nations, including the United States and all 28 NATO members, contribute forces to ISAF. These forces broke Taliban momentum and trained additional Afghan National Security Forces (ANSF). The ANSF are now increasingly assuming responsibility for security on the timeline committed to at the 2010 NATO Summit in Lisbon, and renewed at the Summit in Chicago, by the United States, our NATO allies, ISAF partners, and the Government of Afghanistan. The nations contributing to ISAF will continue to support Afghanistan on its path towards self-reliance in security, improved governance, and economic and social development. This path will prevent Afghanistan from again becoming a safe haven for terrorists that threaten Afghanistan, the region, and the world.[1]

The U.S. mission in Afghanistan includes military, diplomatic, and development programs, personnel, and assets. The President's FY 2013 budget provided $96.7 billion in funding for Overseas Contingency Operations (OCO) to the Department of Defense (DoD), Department of State (DOS), and the U.S. Agency for International Development (USAID) to address U.S. national security goals in Afghanistan, Pakistan, and Iraq. Of that amount, $85.6 billion was provided to DoD for Operation Enduring Freedom, and $3.3 billion for DOS and USAID OCO activities for Afghanistan. Because a final decision about the pace of drawdown in Afghanistan has not yet been made, the President's FY 2014 budget includes a placeholder for DoD's 2014 OCO funding, equivalent to the amount provided in the 2013 Budget, or $88.5 billion; and $3.8 billion for DOS and USAID.

---

[1] Posted at http://www.whitehouse.gov/the-press-office/2013/06/14/letter-president-regarding-war-powers-resolution.

Effective interagency collaboration within the oversight community is essential to providing comprehensive reviews of contingency expenditures, to identify whether critical oversight gaps exist, and to recommend actions to address those gaps. Oversight jurisdiction for Afghanistan is a partnership shared by the Inspectors General for the DoD (DoD IG), State (DOS OIG), and USAID (USAID OIG); the Special Inspector General for Afghanistan Reconstruction (SIGAR); the U.S. Army Audit Agency; Naval Audit Service; the U.S. Air Force Audit Agency; and the U.S. Government Accountability Office (GAO). This oversight community is committed to maintaining an effective working relationship to minimize duplication of efforts and to provide comprehensive oversight coverage.

To optimize this commitment, we have established mechanisms to plan, coordinate, report, and share information and results about U.S. activities in Southwest Asia. In this partnership, the two essential coordination and planning mechanisms for audits, evaluations, and inspections are the Southwest Asia Joint Planning Group (SWA JPG) and the Comprehensive Oversight Plan for Southwest Asia (COPSWA).

> The SWA JPG, established by DoD IG in April 2007, allows for coordination and cooperation among the oversight organizations toward the common objectives of providing comprehensive Southwest Asia oversight. The DoD IG chairs this interagency joint planning group, which meets quarterly or more frequently as needed.

> The COPSWA is an annual plan that incorporates the planned and ongoing work of several DoD and civilian oversight agencies. It includes descriptions of oversight projects that directly affect efforts in Afghanistan and other Southwest Asia countries within the U.S. Central Command's (USCENTCOM) area of responsibility.

Because of the significance of ongoing U.S. missions in Afghanistan, during FY 2012, the SWA JPG established two subgroups to develop a Joint Strategic Oversight Plan for Afghanistan to include in the COPSWA. These subgroups agreed to meet each year to update the plan. The subgroup chaired by SIGAR, led an effort to update the plan for Afghanistan Reconstruction issues. The subgroup chaired by DoD IG, led an effort to update the plan for Other Than Reconstruction issues in Afghanistan. The joint plan was also coordinated with the remaining oversight stakeholder agencies.

SWA JPG Oversight Agency for the FY 2014 Joint Strategic Oversight Plan for Afghanistan	Reconstruction Subgroup	Other Than Reconstruction Subgroup
Special Inspector General for Afghanistan Reconstruction	Chair	
U.S. Agency for International Development OIG	√	
Department of Defense OIG	√	Chair
Department of State OIG	√	√
U.S. Army Audit Agency		√
Oversight Stakeholder Agencies for Coordination: Naval Audit Service, U.S. Air Force Audit Agency, and U.S. Government Accountability Office		

Objectives of Oversight

- Promote accountability, integrity, economy, efficiency, and effectiveness.

- Identify, deter, and investigate fraud, waste, and abuse.

- Support the improvement of contingency business operations, including contracting, logistics, and financial management.

- Support the reform of acquisition and support processes.

- Ensure the safety and needs of civilians, Service members, and their families.

- Provide insight and recommendations to agency and military leadership and Congress, and keep the public informed.

Goals of Oversight

Be relevant, responsive, balanced, and enabling by responding to the needs of agency and military leadership through timely and value added oversight, and by providing assurance to Congress and American taxpayers that the funds provided to support contingency operations in Afghanistan are used correctly and efficiently.

Oversight is a Force-Multiplier

- Supporting military commanders by identifying challenges in critical operations and identifying funds commanders can put to better use to support the operations.

- Supporting the military, civilians, and contractors by identifying life and safety risks and identifying whether they have the necessary equipment, training, and resources to conduct missions within acceptable risks.

- Supporting senior leadership by providing independent, reliable, understandable, and usable reporting to internal and external organizations on the use of funds provided to achieve the national goals of the United States in Afghanistan.

Planning Tools of Oversight

- Strategic: Joint Strategic Oversight Plan for Afghanistan = "the Why" we do the work
  (sometimes noted as the strategic questions to be answered or big picture focus)

- Operational: COPSWA = "the What"
  (oversight project objectives and milestones)

- Tactical: Individual oversight project guides or plans = "the How"
  (methodology)

Risk-Based Planning Process

The oversight community uses a risk-based planning process that includes conducting outreach with congressional representatives, department and agency leadership, USCENTCOM, and senior military and civilian leadership in Afghanistan. Agency leaders in each of the oversight components meet with various senior officials responsible for the significant operations and programs in their respective departments and agencies to include financial, acquisition/contracting, logistics, transportation, and military operations.

We regularly review department, agency, and commanders' strategic documents related to Afghanistan. We also review testimony presented by senior leadership, identify management and program challenges, and evaluate information gathered during our collective oversight work. This framework of information assists in targeting future oversight efforts by identifying existing and emerging systematic management challenges faced by the departments, agencies, commanders, and senior civilian leaders in Afghanistan. Individually and collectively, the members of the SWA JPG continuously assess risk areas to make decisions on relative oversight areas and projects.

Oversight Planning Considerations

In February 2013, GAO reported that since FY 2002, U.S. costs reported for U.S. military, U.S. diplomatic, and reconstruction and relief operations in Afghanistan exceeded $500 billion, and that significant oversight will be needed to help ensure visibility over the cost and progress of these efforts.[2]

♦   Reconstruction Programs and Challenges

In its April 2013 Quarterly Report to Congress, SIGAR reported that since 2002, Congress has provided nearly $93 billion to rebuild Afghanistan. As of March 31, 2013, more than $54 billion has gone to build the Afghan National Army and the Afghan National Police. A stable security environment is vital for the survival and growth of a democratic, non-extremist Afghanistan. The NATO Training Mission-Afghanistan/Combined Security Transition Command-Afghanistan (NTM-A/CSTC-A) used the funds to provide training, purchase equipment, build army and police facilities, and pay salaries as well as operation and maintenance costs.

The United States also provided nearly $23 billion to improve governance and foster economic development in Afghanistan. Most of the assistance for governance and rule of law programs comes through USAID's Economic Support Fund and the State Department's International Narcotics, Control and Law Enforcement account.

Since 2010, the United States and other donors agreed in principle to provide more government-to-government funding—or direct assistance—to help the Government of the Islamic Republic of Afghanistan (GIRoA) institutions build the capacity to manage funds and deliver services. However, the international donor community made this aid conditional on the GIRoA tackling endemic corruption, demonstrating that it has the capacity to manage these funds in a transparent manner, and providing detailed action plans showing how it intends to use development assistance.

---

[2] GAO Report, "Afghanistan: Key Oversight Issues," (GAO-13-218SP, February 11, 2013). GAO reviewed estimates developed by the Congressional Research Service and Special Inspector General for Afghanistan Reconstruction, as well as obligations data provided by DoD and allotment data provided by the Departments of Justice and State. While allotment data are available for U.S. reconstruction and relief efforts in Afghanistan, specific funding figures of U.S. military operations in Afghanistan do not exist because funding provided to DoD for military operations is generally appropriated by operation, not country. Specifically, DoD received funding for Operation Enduring Freedom, which includes Afghanistan.

♦ Other Than Reconstruction Programs and Challenges

DoD IG has identified health care as one of the critical management and performance challenges facing the Department.[3] The military health care system provides services to approximately 9.5 million beneficiaries, including active duty personnel and their families. Of special concern is the proper care and support to the thousands of soldiers, sailors, airmen and Marines wounded in Operations Iraqi and Enduring Freedom combat actions. Medical care for military personnel is expected to increase in the next several years, especially in the areas of rehabilitation and transition care. It is critical for DoD IG to maintain vigorous oversight of the health and safety challenges facing the Department, to ensure that wounded warriors receive high-quality health care and that DoD health care dollars are spent wisely.

During an April 10, 2013, Congressional hearing,[4] DoD IG testified that U.S. and Coalition forces were conducting a phased withdrawal from Afghanistan. Along with the withdrawal of military personnel is the complex withdrawal of DoD equipment. Approximately 35,000 vehicles, numerous helicopters and aircraft, and 95,000 shipping containers will have to be flown out by air or transported overland to seaports for return to the United States.

Oversight will continue during FY 2014 of activities related to the transition from a military-led to a civilian-led U.S. mission in Afghanistan. The withdrawal of U.S. forces and base closures may impede the ability of the oversight agencies and contracting officer representatives to visit project field sites to conduct oversight of service and construction contracts and to monitor the progress of transition and sustainment activities.

This plan describes 11 strategic oversight issues and associated focus areas, and is presented in two sections:

Section 1. Reconstruction
1. Building the Capacity and Capabilities of the Afghan National Security Forces and Administering and Maintaining Accountability of the Afghanistan Security Forces Fund
2. Building Afghan Governance Capacity
3. Sustaining U.S. Investment in Afghan Institutions and Infrastructure
4. Executing and Sustaining Counternarcotics Programs
5. Implementing Anti-Corruption Initiatives
6. Planning, Coordinating, and Providing Stewardship of Direct and Indirect Assistance Funds and Programs
7. Awarding and Administering Reconstruction Contracts

Section 2. Other Than Reconstruction
8. Health and Safety
9. Retrograde and Property Management
10. Contract Management and Oversight
11. Transition Planning and Execution

---

[3] DoD Office of Inspector General Semiannual Report to the Congress, October 1, 2012, through March 31, 2013.
[4] Committee on Oversight and Government Reform Hearing on "U.S. Foreign Assistance: What Oversight Mechanisms are in Place to Ensure Accountability?" April 10, 2013.

Section 1. Reconstruction

Since 2002, the United States has appropriated nearly $93 billion[5] to reconstruct and develop Afghanistan, which ranks among the world's poorest countries, with an annual per capita Gross Domestic Product of less than $550. In addition to widespread illiteracy, poor health systems, weak institutions, and pervasive corruption, the country's social and economic prospects have suffered from decades of civil war, Soviet occupation, and ongoing insurgency and terrorism.

Uses of U.S. reconstruction funds have included the core task of building and sustaining the Afghan National Security Forces (ANSF), promoting governance and rule of law, supporting anticorruption and counternarcotics initiatives, and fostering economic development.

Execution of the reconstruction mission will change dramatically in the years ahead. The exit of U.S. combat forces and most of their support network will, as in Iraq, entail a shift of operational responsibility from DoD to DOS, which also coordinates with USAID. Meanwhile, the closing of U.S. bases and the steadily shrinking "bubbles" of U.S.-provided security and medical evacuation services will complicate and constrain management and oversight of U.S.-funded reconstruction projects.

In this setting, the effectiveness and sustainability of the ANSF and the Afghan Public Protection Force—the state-sanctioned successor to the banned private security companies—take on increased criticality. The reduced U.S. footprint and the promised increase in the portion of U.S. and other international assistance, some of which also involves U.S. funds, directly into the Afghan national budget heightens the importance of increased ministerial capacity, anticorruption initiatives, agreed-upon metrics of progress, and accountability within the GIRoA.

A comparison of this document with the FY 2013 plan will show that the 13 strategic issues previously identified for Reconstruction have been consolidated in FY 2014 to 7 in the interest of logical clarity and to better fit with the concerns of the transfer of greater security and other responsibilities to the GIRoA. These seven strategic issues for FY 2014 continue to fall under four main reconstruction issues:

- ❖ Security
- ❖ Governance and Development
- ❖ Counternarcotics and Law Enforcement/Rule of Law
- ❖ Cross-cutting

---

[5] This and other monetary data are as reported in SIGAR's *Quarterly Report to the United States Congress,* April 30, 2013, posted at www.sigar mil/pdf/quarterlyreports/2013-04-30qr.pdf.

❖ *Security*

Increasing the capability of the ANSF and improving Afghan security is one of four main themes of the United States Government Integrated Civilian–Military Campaign Plan for Support to Afghanistan.[6] The purpose of the strategy is to develop the capacity and capability of the ANSF so that coalition forces can fully transition security responsibilities to the GIRoA by the end of FY 2014.

1. Building the Capacity and Capabilities of the Afghan National Security Forces and Administering and Maintaining Accountability of the Afghanistan Security Forces Fund

Why is this issue important? The ANSF is comprised of the Afghan National Army and the Afghan National Police. The ANSF is a critical pillar for establishing security and stability in Afghanistan. Following the removal of the Taliban from power in 2001, U.S. and coalition partners have focused on establishing an effective, independent, and sustainable ANSF. The long-term goal is to build and develop an ANSF that is nationally respected; professional; ethnically balanced; democratically accountable; organized, trained and equipped to meet the security needs of the country; and increasingly funded from GIRoA revenue.

Risks associated with building the capacity and capabilities of the ANSF include defining requirements, acquisition planning, training, financial management and accountability, and corruption. Sustainment challenges include developing literacy and vocational skills and building institutional capabilities, controls, and processes for effective performance by the Afghan Ministries of Defense and Interior.

As of March 31, 2013, Congress had appropriated more than $54 billion—more than half of all U.S. dollars appropriated for Afghanistan reconstruction since FY 2002—to develop the ANSF. The bulk of this funding, $52.75 billion, has been directed to the Afghanistan Security Forces Fund (ASFF), which was established in 2005. The FY 2013 appropriation for the ASFF was $5.12 billion. Accountability over this fund, which is tracked by DoD through pseudo-foreign military sales case accounts established for each appropriation,[7] is paramount to ensure its proper use to train, equip, and sustain the ANSF.

Key Questions:

- To what extent has DoD established requirements for Afghan security assistance and planned acquisitions that align with Afghan security force structure, unit activations and deployments, and Afghan sustainment capabilities?

---

[6] This plan, dated February 2011, provides strategic guidance from the U.S. Chief of Mission and the Commander of U.S. Forces-Afghanistan to U.S. civilian and military personnel in Afghanistan on the focus and execution of the mission through 2014.

[7] In general, ASFF funds associated with pseudo-foreign military sales cases retain the limitations placed on them when appropriated. Such funds must be obligated prior to the appropriation expiring and expended prior to cancellation of the appropriation.

- Is the ANSF making sufficient progress in building capacity and capabilities needed to fully assume security responsibilities, and to maintain accountability for the equipment and supplies they receive?
- To what extent has DoD determined the capabilities that the ANSF will require from the U.S. and coalition post-2014 to enable them to successfully carry out the lead security operations role?
- Has DoD properly administered and maintained accountability over the use of funds in the ASFF?
- Has DoD developed the capability of the Ministry of Defense and Ministry of Interior to effectively manage and account for direct funding received from the ASFF?

FOCUS AREAS

➤ Extent of DoD planning for and execution of equipping and logistics support of ANSF

➤ Progress in developing ANSF into an operationally independent and sustainable security force

➤ Vetting of construction requirements for base transfers, force-structure changes, and sustainability of facilities transferring to GIRoA

➤ Verifying instructors, curriculum, and outcomes of literacy, vocational, and leadership training

➤ Progress of training ANSF to assume security responsibilities

➤ Progress of ANSF to perform and sustain capabilities for command and control, financial management, logistics, and medical support

➤ Whether ANSF is maintaining accountable control over equipment and supplies

➤ Verifying sufficiency of controls over ASFF transactions

➤ Evaluation of controls over ASFF pseudo-foreign military sales cases

❖ *Governance and Development*

The U.S. reconstruction strategy emphasizes strengthening Afghan governance and supporting sustainable, inclusive growth. Since FY 2002, Congress has provided nearly $23 billion to build Afghanistan's governing institutions and foster economic and social development. This money has gone into a number of funds and supported a myriad of programs managed by USAID, DOS, and DoD, including programs related to building governance capacity, promoting democracy and civil society, growing the economy, building or rehabilitating infrastructure, expanding access to education and health care, and boosting agricultural production. FY 2013 appropriations total $644 million.

The three largest funds and programs during FY 2002 to FY 2013 are the Economic Support Fund, Commander's Emergency Response Program, and Afghanistan Infrastructure Fund.

They have accounted for $19.7 billion, or about 86 percent, of all funds appropriated for governance and development.

2. Building Afghan Governance Capacity

Why is this issue important? A key focus of U.S. capacity building efforts is developing the budgeting capability within Afghan national and sub-national governmental institutions. This capability is reflected in developing governmental budgets and having government ministries follow through with execution of their respective budgets within the proper budget cycle. Strengthening this capacity will help the GIRoA make responsible decisions about the use of its finite resources, one of the fundamental requirements of self-governance.

Under Afghanistan's Fiscal Year 1392[8] National Budget (December 2012 - December 2013)[9], about 72 percent of the government's operating budget was for salaries of government employees. A large portion of the GIRoA's wages and salaries were paid through the Afghanistan Reconstruction Trust Fund, Law and Order Trust Fund for Afghanistan, and ASFF. The United States was the largest donor to the Afghanistan Reconstruction Trust Fund and Law and Order Trust Fund. Challenges faced by the GIRoA include Afghan pay and grade reform, merit based hiring, and improvements in financial management.

In addition, a key priority of the U.S. reconstruction strategy is to support inclusive and constitutional Afghan presidential elections in 2014 and parliamentary elections in 2015. The United States and the international community see free and fair presidential and parliamentary elections as fundamental to establishing a government that is legitimate in the eyes of the majority of the Afghan people, thereby contributing to political stability. U.S. funding and assistance has provided support to programs at the provincial, district, and local levels to strengthen the Afghan electoral system; to train political parties, coalitions and entities; and to provide voter and civic education.

Key Questions:

- To what extent has the GIRoA developed financial management capacity at both the national and sub-national levels?

- What steps have been taken to ensure that lessons learned from prior capacity-building programs at the sub-national levels have been incorporated into the design and implementation of follow-on capacity-building programs?

---

[8] Afghanistan follows the solar Heiri calendar, which began in 622 A.D. in the Gregorian calendar and runs from March 21-March 20. The Afghan government's fiscal year had been the same as the solar year, but fiscal year 1391 ran only from March 21, 2012, to December 20, 2012, to better align with donors' fiscal calendars. This one-time, nine-month fiscal year bridged the change to a new Afghan fiscal year that now runs from December 21-December 20. Afghan fiscal year 1392 began on December 21, 2012 and will end on December 20, 2013. SIGAR converts Heiri solar years to Gregorian equivalents.
[9] Islamic Republic of Afghanistan Ministry of Finance 1392 National Budget.

- To what extent has the GIRoA succeeded in implementing civil-service and pay reforms, and what actions are planned or under way to address remaining implementation challenges and impediments?
- Has U.S. assistance achieved intended outcomes and sustainable electoral reforms, and to what extent have preparations been made for administering the Afghan 2014 elections?

FOCUS AREAS

➤ Capacity of GIRoA to prepare a comprehensive budget

➤ Capacity of the ministries to spend funds and operate in accordance with approved budgets

➤ Whether U.S-funded programs include provisions for transitioning responsibilities from external technical experts to Afghan civil servants

➤ Whether USAID incorporated lessons learned into capacity-building programs for sub-national levels of government

➤ GIRoA's progress and challenges in implementing land-reform initiatives, and whether USAID assistance is focused on these challenges

➤ Whether USAID's Afghan Civil Service Support Program has achieved expected outcomes regarding merit-based hiring and promotion, and pay-and-grade reform

➤ Challenges for implementing merit-based hiring and promotion, and pay-and-grade reform; and whether USAID's assistance is focused on these challenges

➤ Extent of the GIRoA's implementation of the Verified Payroll Program for making salary payments

➤ Whether USAID's electoral programs are achieving intended outcomes and will be completed in time for the 2014 elections

➤ Challenges in preparation for the 2014 elections, and whether U.S. assistance is focused on the most critical areas to prepare the GIRoA for them

➤ Sustainability of capacity-building efforts within the Afghan Independent Election Commission and electoral reforms

➤ Extent that stabilization, development, and rule-of-law programs are achieving goals and objectives, and what reevaluation actions were taken in response to program metrics and outcomes achieved

3. Sustaining U.S. Investment in Afghan Institutions and Infrastructure

Why is this issue important? Failure by the U.S. Government to adequately address the capacity of the GIRoA to sustain U.S. reconstruction programs and investments will not only waste U.S. taxpayers' funds, but undermine local government credibility and impede progress in reconstruction and stabilization.

Key Questions:

- To what extent have U.S. reconstruction programs and investments taken into account the capacity of the GIRoA to sustain these programs and investments?

- To what extent has the GIRoA made progress in generating revenues to fund governmental operations?

- Has U.S. assistance been used effectively to implement Afghan customs and tax reform initiatives?

FOCUS AREAS

➢ Whether sustainability was integrated into development programs consistent with the USAID Administrator's Sustainability Guidance for USAID to Afghanistan

➢ Actions taken by the U.S. Government to identify gaps and address sustainment issues with development programs

➢ Extent that the U.S. Government developed requirements and programmed funds to support sustainment of Afghan programs and infrastructure investments

➢ Afghan Ministry of Finance's progress and challenges in implementing customs and tax reforms, and whether USAID's assistance is focused on these challenges

➢ Extent that Afghanistan and Pakistan earned revenue by improperly charging import duties and taxes on exempt U.S. Government shipments, and actions the U.S. Government has taken to seek refunds

➢ GIRoA's progress in commercializing the public-utility sector and generating revenues to fund continuing operations

❖ *Counternarcotics and Law Enforcement/Rule of Law*

Congress appropriated $6.39 billion for counternarcotics and law-enforcement/rule-of-law initiatives in Afghanistan from FY 2002 through March 30, 2013. FY 2013 appropriations were $378 million. The bulk of appropriated funds were for the State Department's International Narcotics Control and Law Enforcement Fund (INCLE) and DoD's Drug Interdiction and Counter-Drug Activities. INCLE appropriations have also included funds for the Administration of Justice, Justice Sector Support, and Corrections System Support Programs carried out in Afghanistan.

4. Executing and Sustaining Counternarcotics Programs

Why is this issue important? Afghanistan produces 90 percent of the world's opium.[10] The illegal drug trade provides income for Afghan farmers, bribes for government officials, profits to dealers, and revenues for insurgents. By undermining the rule of law and funding insurgents, the opium trade constitutes a major challenge to Afghanistan's reconstruction. The DoD counternarcotics appropriation primarily funds intelligence

---

[10] SIGAR Quarterly Report to the U.S. Congress, April 30, 2013; posted at http://www.sigar.mil/pdf/quarterlyreports/2013-04-30qr.pdf.

operations to detect and monitor drug trafficking, air mobility and training for the Afghanistan counternarcotics police, and facilities, training, and equipment for the Afghanistan counternarcotics border police.

Key Questions:

- Has U.S. assistance for Afghanistan succeeded in achieving the goals and objectives of the counternarcotics strategy?

- How capable is the GIRoA of assuming a lead role and sustaining progress in counternarcotics operations?

FOCUS AREAS

➢ Whether counternarcotics programs are achieving intended outcomes, and identifying challenges and impediments to sustained progress

➢ U.S. agencies' monitoring and evaluation of counternarcotics programs, and of reevaluation actions taken in response to program metrics and outcomes achieved

➢ Extent of GIRoA preparations to sustain counternarcotics program

5. Implementing Anti-Corruption Initiatives

Why is this issue important? A major part of the U.S. reconstruction strategy is focused on expanding Afghans' access to justice and promoting the rule of law. U.S. support for the rule of law in Afghanistan focuses on efforts to provide Afghans with meaningful access to fair, efficient, and transparent justice. The U.S. Government is also funding programs to develop Afghan capacity to effectively investigate and prosecute national security and major counternarcotics cases.

Key Questions:

- To what extent has the GIRoA implemented anticorruption programs within its ministries and made progress in deterring corruption by investigating, prosecuting, sanctioning, or removing corrupt officials from office, and by implementing financial-transparency and accountability measures for government institutions and officials?

- To what extent have rule-of-law programs improved Afghanistan's justice and corrections systems and increased public access to justice?

FOCUS AREAS

➢ Extent to which GIRoA's implementation of anticorruption programs within its ministries is consistent with guidance from the Afghan High Office of Oversight for Anti-Corruption

➢ Criteria and reliability of information that DOS and USAID used to certify that the GIRoA is reducing corruption in order to meet defined aid restrictions

> ➤ Whether U.S. assistance to the GIRoA for anticorruption programs is achieving intended outcomes and is focused in areas of greatest impact for achieving strategic objectives

> ➤ DOS monitoring and evaluation of training under rule-of-law programs

> ➤ Number of trained Afghan legal professionals and number still employed by the GIRoA in the justice sector

> ➤ Progress and outcomes of rule-of-law programs to develop capacity within Afghan justice institutions at the national and provincial levels

> ➤ Whether the DOS Bureau of International Narcotics and Law Enforcement Affairs has effectively administered funds for prison construction and operations of the Afghan correctional system

❖ *Cross-Cutting*

Crosscutting issues arise from supporting activities that span multiple sectors and subsectors of Afghan reconstruction. They are typically not linked to a particular reconstruction appropriation. Examples include financial management, contracting, staffing, and security of reconstruction-mission activities.

6. Planning, Coordinating, and Providing Stewardship of Direct and Indirect Assistance Funds and Programs

Why are these issues important? The upfront planning and coordination of U.S. assistance programs is an area prone to weaknesses. Previous audits and inspections identified the need for more informed tradeoffs between risk and rewards in determining which programs to execute; better defined program objectives and metrics; increased coordination of programs; and integration of Afghan sustainability into program design and implementation. Furthermore, some programs are not showing progress in delivering intended outcomes and may be at risk of failing.

Key Questions:

- To what extent has the U.S. Government vetted and designed direct- and indirect-assistance programs to ensure they are necessary, achievable, and sustainable?

- Has the U.S. coordinated programs to achieve unity of effort with the GIRoA and the international donor community?

- To what extent are GIRoA ministries providing stewardship of direct assistance funds and achieving favorable outcomes from programs funded through direct assistance?

FOCUS AREAS

> ➤ Whether DoD, USAID, and DOS have established processes to vet and design assistance programs to ensure that they are necessary, achievable, and sustainable

➢ Where U.S. Government economic-development programs rank on a high/low continuum of risk-to-reward, and what results they achieved at what cost

➢ Whether DoD, USAID, and DOS are fully coordinating projects to prevent duplication and to achieve mutually supporting outcomes to deliver optimum benefits

➢ Extent of U.S. Government coordination of assistance projects with the GIRoA and the international community to prevent duplication and achieve unity of effort

➢ Whether DoD, DOS and USAID are maintaining sufficient oversight of the use of direct assistance funds to ensure the GIRoA is exercising proper stewardship

➢ Whether the GIRoA is exercising financial management of direct-assistance funds and achieving expected outcomes for programs funded through direct assistance

7. Awarding and Administering Reconstruction Contracts

Why are these issues important? The risks associated with contingency contracting remain high. We plan to continue our oversight to make sure the government is paying fair and reasonable prices and not getting overbilled by contractors for items and services procured. The drawdown of military forces will make it more difficult to provide the forces needed for contracting officer representatives to monitor contracts. Also, the constant rotation of contracting personnel makes it a challenge to maintain a sufficient number of personnel with the right qualifications to provide adequate oversight. These inherent risks are likely to continue despite the improvements that DOS, DoD, and USAID have made. Additionally, USAID has a large backlog of contracts requiring a financial audit of contractor's incurred costs before the contracts can be closed.

Key Question:

• To what extent did DoD, DOS, and USAID award contracts competitively and administer contracts for Afghanistan's reconstruction in a manner to ensure costs are controlled and contractors remain on schedule and perform as required?

FOCUS AREAS

➢ Whether DoD, USAID, and DOS are using acquisition strategies that best promote competition, minimize risk, control cost, and achieve favorable performance outcomes

➢ Whether GIRoA contracts financed by the U.S. Government are awarded and administered in accordance with agreed-upon standards and procedures

➢ Whether the U.S. Government obtained fair and reasonable prices on goods and services purchased, and whether they were properly delivered and accounted for throughout the acquisition process

➢ Whether amounts billed to the U.S. Government for contracts and grants in support of Afghanistan reconstruction were allowable, allocable, and reasonable

➢ Whether DoD, USAID, and DOS are fully accounting for and managing the disposition of contractor-managed, government-owned equipment from awarded contracts

Section 2. Other Than Reconstruction

Presidentially directed force reductions in Afghanistan will continue to the 34,000 level by February 12, 2014. The withdrawal of U.S. forces and resulting base closures may impede the ability of U.S. oversight agencies and contracting officer representatives to visit project field sites to conduct oversight of service and construction contracts and to monitor the progress of transition and sustainment activities. However, through the end of 2014, oversight efforts will continue, consistent with the security posture of U.S. forces and the Command's ability to provide support.

As of March 31, 2013, cumulative appropriations for the Afghanistan Security Force Fund (ASFF) were approximately $52.75 billion for DoD to train and equip an Afghan National Security Force (ANSF) of 352,000 personnel. The FY 2013 funding level for the ASFF of more than $5.12 billion is a decrease of more than $6 billion from the $11.2 billion initially appropriated in FY 2012. Reprogramming activity and rescissions reduced the FY 2012 appropriation amount from $11.2 billion to $9.2 billion. This reduced funding may reflect the shift in emphasis from building the Afghan security forces, largely accomplished, towards professionalizing and sustaining them.

The FY 2014 foreign assistance budget justification[11] includes a request for about $2.2 billion to support programs for Afghanistan; specifically, approximately $1.5 billion for Overseas Contingency Operations (OCO) and about $749 million base funding for enduring/core programs. This represents a strategic approach that is crucial to achieving U.S. Government goals in Afghanistan. Core resources will focus on enduring needs and aspects of programs whose scope and nature are focused on long-term, sustainable development. OCO resources will be used for immediate and extraordinary needs that are critical to successful security and political transitions, as well as to ensuring that Afghanistan has the necessary economic foundations to shift to a market driven economy.

External impacts to the Afghanistan theater of operations include:

- U.S. national fiscal challenges,

- Reduced Defense budget,

- Overdependence on outsourced capability,

- Rapidly changing environment and missions, and

- Need for more precise requirements generation process and improved execution management.

---

[11] "Fiscal Year 2014 Congressional Budget Justification for Foreign Operations – Annex: Regional Perspective", pages 534 and 732; posted at http://www.state.gov/documents/organization/208291.pdf.

Concept of Operations

There are multiple complex and challenging operations ongoing in an environment of competing and, sometimes, conflicting goals that require DoD leadership attention:

- ✓ Maintain the national security goals;
- ✓ Safety of the force;
- ✓ Force drawdown;
- ✓ Base realignment, closure, and transfer to the GIRoA;
- ✓ Redeployment, Retrograde, Redistribution, Return, and Disposal (R4D) of equipment and supplies - removing excess rolling stock (vehicles and associated enablers) and supplies (both standard and non-standard stock supplies);
- ✓ Reduction of contracts and contractors; and
- ✓ Transition from DoD to DOS.

A comparison of this document with the FY 2013 plan will observe that the nine strategic issues identified last year for Other Than Reconstruction have been consolidated in FY 2014 to four issues to better fit with drawdown concerns relating to U.S. personnel, property, fiduciary responsibility, and transition activities.

8. Health and Safety

Why is this issue important? The health, safety and security of U.S. personnel supporting overseas military contingency operations and diplomatic missions are among the highest priorities for oversight. As of April 2013, the U.S had about 67,000 military personnel in Afghanistan supported by about 110,000 civilians and contractors.[12] In addition, U.S. Embassy – Kabul, accounted for approximately 1,200 civilian personnel in Kabul and in the field.[13]

In the areas of health, personnel safety and physical security, oversight organizations will review whether: 1) personnel are provided the highest quality and safest equipment, safe basic life support, and the proper security protection within the criteria of regulation, policy, and reasonable affordability; 2) unauthorized, illegal, or potentially life-threatening activities are effectively detected and deterred; and 3) the level of health, safety and quality have been achieved by risk assessment, identified requirements, and proper oversight.

From 2011 to 2012, there were 12 electrical and fire-related deaths of U.S. personnel in Operation Enduring Freedom.[14] Previous DoD IG assessments uncovered multiple and recurring serious electrical and fire protection violations in DoD-controlled facilities in Afghanistan. In April and May 2012, DoD IG conducted assessments at Kandahar Air

---

[12] U.S. Forces-Afghanistan, "Joint Personnel Status Report," April 28, 2013.

[13] Chief of Mission – Embassy Kabul.

[14] As reported by Task Force Power which has the roles and responsibilities to inspect fire and electrical life, health, and safety hazards throughout the Combined/Joint Operations Area – Afghanistan (CJOA-A).

Field[15] that identified more than 400 deficiencies related to life, health, and safety. Assessments at the Bagram Air Field[16] in July and August 2012 identified more than 600 life, health, and safety deficiencies. Several of the findings required immediate corrective action due to their severity. Assessments such as those conducted by the DoD IG to determine if U.S.-occupied facilities are in compliance with applicable standards are essential for the protection and safety of the warfighter.

Another critical area of safety is the health care and welfare support provided to personnel returning from Afghanistan. This support includes proper medical support for wounded warriors; families of personnel killed in action and of wounded warriors; post deployment assessments; and assistance with transition to the next life cycle for those who have served.

Key Questions:

- To what extent has the construction of U.S.-funded and occupied facilities complied with electrical and fire protection standards specified by DoD and DOS?

- To what extent has DOS implemented effective security and safety support for embassy personnel?

- To what extent are the military redeploying personnel properly?

- Have the military services set up adequate processes to properly support wounded warriors and their families, to include assistance with transition to civilian status or reintegration into military service?

FOCUS AREAS

➢ Physical Security
➢ Personnel Security and Safety
➢ Health Care and Welfare

9. Retrograde and Property Management

Why is this issue important? In his February 13, 2013, State of the Union Address, President Obama announced that, "over the next year, another 34,000 American troops will come home from Afghanistan. This drawdown will continue and by the end of next year, our war in Afghanistan will be over."[17] The U.S. drawdown from Afghanistan

---

[15] On June 29, 2012, DoD OIG issued two Notices of Concern to appropriate DoD officials relating to the inspections conducted at Kandahar Air Field. One notice related to the inspection of compliance with electrical standards, and the other for compliance with fire protection standards.

[16] On October 10, 2012, DoD OIG issued two Notices of Concern to appropriate DoD officials relating to the inspections conducted at Bagram Air Field. One notice related to the inspection of compliance with electrical standards, and the other for compliance with fire protection standards.

[17] Remarks by the President in the State of the Union Address, February 13, 2013. Posted at http://www.whitehouse.gov/photos-and-video/video/2013/02/12/2013-state-union-address-0#transcript.

continues. As of April 2013, there were roughly 67,000 troops and millions of pieces of equipment in Afghanistan.

This rapid redeployment of forces results in an immense amount of deployed equipment and property requiring intensive management. Critical processes are needed to identify, account for, safeguard, and determine the optimum disposition of materiel—considering both cost effectiveness and the required reset of CONUS-based DoD units; opportunities to transfer equipment to DOS embassy operations; and practicality of appropriate transfers to the GIRoA or other nations. In addition, maintaining adequate visibility and accountability during intra- and inter-theater transportation contributes to keeping sensitive items out of the hands of insurgents while continuing to fill critical needs of U.S. forces and personnel.

USCENTCOM subordinate commands have developed policies, processes, and programs to manage the retrograde effort, including but not limited to clean sweep operations, USCENTCOM Materiel Recovery Element personnel who assist commands prepare for base closure, and Found-on-Installation initiatives. As of April 2013, USCENTCOM has retrograded equipment for many redeploying military units. However, in conjunction with the drawdown of personnel through the end of 2014, a massive amount of materiel remains to be retrograded.

According to U.S. Forces-Afghanistan (USFOR-A), as of April 30, 2013, the cost for retrograde operations was about $1.2 billion. USFOR-A estimates additional retrograde costs through December 2014 will be $6.9 billion.

Key Questions:

- Has DoD sufficiently planned and developed robust management controls to execute the redeployment, retrograde, redistribution, return, and disposal of materiel (R4D)?

- Are disposition decisions supported by adequate cost/benefit analyses and/or critical CONUS requirements?

- Has DoD accurately identified and quantified the amount of materiel for retrograde processing?

- Do management control processes governing R4D adequately mitigate the risk of loss during transportation to the final destination—Intra-theater, inter-theater, ground and air lines of communication (GLOC and ALOC)?

- To what extent is the military shipping controlled materials and munitions properly?

- Are DoD and DOS coordinating efforts to identify and properly account for equipment that will be transferred from DoD to DOS?

- Does DOS have adequate policies and procedures to ensure that equipment transferred from DoD is properly accounted for?

FOCUS AREAS

➢ Redeployment, Retrograde, Redistribution, Return, and Disposal (R4D)
  o Rolling stock
  o Equipment and supplies
  o Medical equipment and supplies (including hazmat and pharmacy items)
  o Ammunition
  o Classified/sensitive items

➢ Property disposal

➢ Air and ground lines of communication (ALOC and GLOC Transportation)

➢ Repatriating equipment loaned to coalition partners

➢ Readiness of support functions/activities

  o Army Field Support Brigade Redistribution Property Assistance Team (RPAT) Yards (Class VII and other Theater Provided Equipment) and Sustainment Brigades to support the R4D

  o Defense Logistics Agency managed activities, such as wholesale supply depot management and fuel management

  o Sierra Army Depot for the sorting and storage of retrograde non-rolling stock

➢ Container management

➢ Property accountability
  o Unit equipment
  o Loaned equipment
  o In-transit visibility
  o Theater provided equipment
  o Non-standard supplies and equipment
  o Weapons
  o Sensitive and classified materiel
    ▪ Night vision devices
    ▪ Radios
  o Excess inventory

➢ DoD to DOS equipment transfers

➢ Policies and processes for closing bases and for the transfer of land and facilities to GIRoA

➢ Disposition of excess real and personal property

10. Contract Management and Oversight

Why is this issue important? DoD and DOS continue to face significant challenges in the area of contract award, oversight, documentation, and administration. Spending on security, transportation, and equipment, among other areas, must continue even as the U.S. draws down in Afghanistan. Weaknesses in financial management of funds earmarked for U.S. operations in Afghanistan have been identified that impact financial reporting, but also the efficiency and effectiveness of business operations. Oversight assists in identifying improvements and efficiencies in the management of contracts and processes by reducing non-productive processes and bureaucracy, targeting affordability and controlling growth, promoting real competition, and improving services' acquisitions.

DoD and DOS have numerous active contracts in Afghanistan, including contracts for information operations, security services, military and embassy/consulate construction, and vehicle maintenance. The Commission on Wartime Contracting in Iraq and Afghanistan[18] released a final report in August 2011,[19] which found as much as $60 billion of waste and fraud in wartime contracts for the two wars. Oversight components have determined that contract requirements were frequently not well-defined and that the contracting arrangements were often not the most appropriate for ensuring the efficient and effective use of resources.

Further, oversight efforts found that contract oversight responsibility was given to a contracting workforce, including the contracting officers' representatives, that was not properly sized, sufficiently trained, nor possessing the experience necessary to manage the complexities of these acquisitions. For these reasons, contract management and oversight remains a high risk area and continues to be vulnerable to increased fraud, waste, and mismanagement of taxpayer funds.

Although there has been increased awareness of the need for trained contracting officer representatives in theater, adequate surveillance of contractor performance in a contingency environment remains a major challenge. With ongoing obligations of significant amounts of funding to contracts in Afghanistan, there is a continued need to assess the use of contractors in support of U.S. military and civilian organizations in Afghanistan, the adequacy of oversight of those contracts, and the controls over funds.

Key Questions:

- To what extent are U.S. government officials properly soliciting, awarding, managing, and administering contracts in accordance with Federal Acquisition Regulations and other applicable guidance?

---

[18] Congress created the independent, bipartisan Commission on Wartime Contracting in Iraq and Afghanistan in 2008 (Public Law 110-181) to assess contingency contracting for reconstruction, logistics, and security functions; examine the extent of waste, fraud, and abuse; and provide recommendations to Congress to improve the structures, policies, and resources for managing the contracting process and contractors.

[19] "Transforming Wartime Contracting: Controlling costs, reducing risks," August 2011. This final report to Congress summarizes the Commission's work since 2008.

- To what extent do contracting officers have adequate controls over purchases of goods and services performed in Afghanistan?

- Is the contract oversight of contractor performance on military construction projects effective?

- To what extent are fees and surcharges charged against the ASFF appropriate and supported?

- To what extent are the Afghan National Army Trust Fund contributions properly managed?

- To what extent are agreements in place with Coalition Forces for shared services?

FOCUS AREAS

- Contract Management
- Contract Closeout
- Logistics Civil Augmentation Program (LOGCAP)
- Drawdown of contracts and contractor employees
- Management of program management contract maintenance facilities and spare parts
- Adequacy of long term acquisition strategies and planning for re-competing contracts
- Vendor pay
- Prompt pay
- Cross Servicing Agreements
- Financial audit of contracts
- Funds control
- Contractor-managed government-owned property
- Disposition of excess contractor-managed government-owned property

11. Transition Planning and Execution

Why is this issue important? By the end of 2014, U.S. policy and related military and diplomatic strategy in Afghanistan will be implemented by complex operations that emphasize:

- providing continued training, equipping, advising and assisting to enable the ANSF to continue leading security operations;

- conducting a phased drawdown of U.S. combat forces in 2013 and 2014;

- transitioning reconstruction and development programs consistent with the size and shape of the post-2014 U.S. security footprint; and

- laying the ground work for an enduring, post-2014 NATO and U.S. support presence in Afghanistan

The U.S. and coalition mission to train and equip the ANSF has changed from force generation to force sustainment. This includes providing materiel support to the ANSF through NTM-A/CSTC-A and, post-2014, through the Office of Security Cooperation-Afghanistan, as well as U.S.-provided enabler capability to ensure the ANSF can operate independently after the withdrawal of U.S. and Coalition combat forces.

The drawdown of U.S. combat forces involves the orderly closing of bases throughout Afghanistan and the selective transfer of land and facilities to GIRoA by December 31, 2014. Closing a base presents significant challenges for DoD, and requires extensive planning to determine DoD transportation capacity and whether appropriate steps are being taken to ensure efficient movement, storage and disposition of assets during the drawdown.

DoD is currently engaged in a large number of construction projects that include buildings, roads, air strips and other infrastructure, to increase Afghanistan's stability, security, and strengthen its economy. Because of the U.S. military drawdown and the transfer of DoD operations to the DOS, it is important to verify the requirements for any new construction, as well as the capability of GIRoA to finish any incomplete construction projects transferred to it at the end of 2014. Further, the ability of GIRoA to maintain completed facilities already transferred is critical.

Finally, the transition from DoD to DOS in Iraq provides many lessons learned that need to be considered as the DoD and DOS prepare for a comparable transition in Afghanistan. Effective transition planning and execution is critical to supporting U.S. and NATO security objectives to build and sustain a unified and sovereign Afghanistan.

Key Questions:

- What progress has been made for the transfer of lead responsibility for security to the ANSF?

- To what extent will DoD have a post-2014 role in Afghanistan?

- To what extent have DoD and DOS developed and implemented a plan for transitioning to a reduced DoD presence in Afghanistan, including establishing an Office of Security Cooperation – Afghanistan, and have key transition and operational challenges been identified?

- To what extent have base closure processes been identified and managed for real property, equipment, and environmental requirements?

- What progress has been made in building the capacity of GIRoA to maintain transferred infrastructure?

FOCUS AREAS

➢ Level and nature of DoD support required for enduring U.S. Embassy operations

➢ Establishment of and support to the Office of Security Cooperation – Afghanistan

➤ Transition planning for U.S. reconstruction and development programs to reflect the reducing U.S. security footprint

➤ Adequacy of the U.S. government's inventory and documentation for the land ownership agreements of any enduring bases

➤ Resolution of DoD contracts: termination, transfer to DOS or transfer to the Afghan Ministries of Defense and Interior, and ANSF

➤ Capacity of the Afghan Ministries of Defense and Interior, and ANSF to manage the contracts transferred to them and any direct financial contributions provided them by the U.S. and the rest of the international community

➤ Capability of GIRoA to maintain the infrastructure DoD transfers to them

➤ Capability of GIRoA to complete unfinished U.S. construction

PAGE INTENTIONALLY LEFT BLANK

Section 1.1. Afghanistan Summary Matrix of FY 2014 Projects

SUMMARY PRORATED OVERSIGHT COVERAGE BY FY 2014 AFGHANISTAN STRATEGIC OVERSIGHT ISSUES
(as of September 1, 2013)

NUMBER OF PROJECTS BY AGENCY FY 2014 STRATEGIC ISSUE	DOD OIG Total	AAA Total	AFAA Total	NAV AUD SVC Total	SIGAR Total	GAO Total	DOS OIG Total	USAID OIG Total	Total Per Issue
RECONSTRUCTION									
1. Building the Capacity and Capabilities of the Afghan National Security Forces and Administering and Maintaining Accountability of the Afghanistan Security Forces Fund	9.5				7.0	1.0			17.5
2. Building Afghan Governance Capacity					8.0		0.3	74.0	82.3
3. Sustaining U.S. Investment in Afghan Institutions and Infrastructure					19.5		0.3	5.0	24.8
4. Executing and Sustaining Counternarcotics Programs					1.0		1.3	1.0	3.3
5. Implementing Anti-Corruption Initiatives					2.5			1.0	3.5
6. Planning, Coordinating, and Providing Stewardship of Direct and Indirect Assistance Funds and Programs	1.0				3.0			1.0	5.0
7. Awarding and Administering Reconstruction Contracts					43.5		0.5	8.0	52.0
OTHER THAN RECONSTRUCTION									
8. Health and Safety		1.0				2.0			3.0
9. Retrograde and Property Management	5.5	4.0	11.0			2.0	1.5		24.0
10. Contract Management and Oversight	6.5	5.0				5.0	3.0	2.0	21.5
11. Transition Planning and Execution	4.5			2.0	0.5	2.0	2.0	1.0	11.5
Total number of projects per agency (a)	27	10	11	2	85	12	9	93	249

NOTE:
(a) A project may cover more than one issue. For example, if a project covers three strategic issues, each issue is prorated a value of 0.3. Total number of projects is rounded and represents the number of projects each ageny has submitted for the FY 2014 COPSWA.

Section 1.2. Afghanistan Projects by Agency and Reference Number

Department of Defense Office of Inspector General

Project	Start	Final	Strategic Issue
COPSWA Ref. No. 668 **Shindand Training Contracts** Objective: Determine whether pilot training contracts for fixed-wing and rotary-wing aircraft at Shindand are properly managed and administered in accordance with Federal and DoD requirements. Specifically, we will determine whether contract requirements are being met and evaluate the effectiveness of contract oversight. (Project: D2013-D000AS-0052.000)	Nov-12	Dec-13	1
COPSWA Ref. No. 905 **Audit of the Surveillance Structure on Contracts Supporting the Afghanistan Rotary Wing Program for the U.S. Transportation Command** Objective: Determine whether U.S. Transportation Command and USCENTCOM officials have adequate oversight of processes and procedures for the contracts. (Project: D2013-D000AS-0001.000)	Oct-12	Nov-13	1 10
COPSWA Ref. No. 906 **Information Operations Assessments in Afghanistan** Objective: Determine whether U.S. Forces-Afghanistan implemented sufficient controls for assessments of Information Operations (Project: D2012-D000JA-0223.000)	Sep-12	Sep-13	10
COPSWA Ref. No. 907 **Contract Oversight of Military Construction Projects for the Special Operations Forces Complexes at Bagram Airfield, Afghanistan** Objective: Determine whether DoD is providing effective oversight of military construction projects in Afghanistan. Specifically, we will determine whether the U.S. Army Corps of Engineers (USACE) is properly monitoring contractor performance and adequately performing quality assurance oversight responsibilities for construction projects for Special Operations Forces at Bagram Airfield. (Project: D2012-D000JO-0221.000)	Sep-12	Sep-13	10

Project	Start	Final	Strategic Issue
COPSWA Ref. No. 908 **Assessment of the U.S. Military and Coalition Efforts to Develop Effective and Sustainable Healthcare Capability for the Afghan National Police (ANP)** Objectives: Determine whether plans to develop effective and sustainable healthcare services to the ANP are sufficiently comprehensive, coordinated with GIRoA, and being implemented so as to meet the timeline for transition goals; advisory resources are sufficient and appropriate in order to develop the healthcare services necessary to support the medical needs of the ANP; and developmental efforts are on schedule and effective in ensuring there is adequate medical capability to provide proper medical support to ANP personnel from the point of injury to the next required level of care. (Project: D2013-D00SPO-0154.000)	Apr-13	Jan-14	1
COPSWA Ref. No. 911 **Assessment of Planning for the Effective Development/Transition of Critical ANSF Enablers to Post-2014 Capabilities** Objectives: Determine whether U.S./Coalition Forces goals, objectives, plans, guidance, and resources are sufficient to develop, manage, and transition critical ANSF operational enablers; what critical enabling task capabilities will require further development beyond 2014; and whether mitigating actions are planned and what they consist of for any post-2014 enabler development. A series of reports are planned for this project. (Project: D2013-D00SPO-0087.000)	Dec-12	Oct-13	1 11
COPSWA Ref. No. 912 **ANP Metrics Product** Objective: Provide a summary of the Afghan National Police readiness to take the lead in Afghanistan security operations relative to U.S. forces withdrawal scheduled for 2014. (Project: D2011-D00SPO-0182.007)	Jun-13	Dec-13	1
COPSWA Ref. No. 913 **Redistribution Property Assistance Team Operations in Afghanistan** Objective: Determine whether Redistribution Property Assistance Teams in Afghanistan have effective procedures in place to process equipment, including prepartion for shipment. (Project: D2013-D000JB-0133.000)	Mar-13	Dec-13	9

Project	Start	Final	Strategic Issue
COPSWA Ref. No. 914 **Examination of Department of Defense Execution of NATO Contributing Countries Donations to Afghan National Army (ANA)Trust Fund for Approved Sustainment Projects, as of September 30, 2012** Objectives: Determine whether Under Secretary of Defense (Comptroller)/Chief Financial Officer fairly presented receipts and expenditures of funds contributed to the ANA Trust Fund and transferred to DoD for execution under the terms of the Memorandum of Understanding Among the United States of America and North Atlantic Treaty Organization and Supreme Headquarters Allied Powers-Europe Regarding Management and Administration of Trust Fund Donations for Support and Sustainment of the ANA. In addition, we will review internal controls over financial reporting and compliance with laws and regulations as it relates to our engagement objective. Our responsibility is to express an opinion based on our examination. (Project: D2013-D000FL-0056.000)	Dec-12	Feb-14	6
COPSWA Ref. No. 915 **Controls Over the Disposition of Equipment at the Defense Logistics Agency Disposition Services in Afghanistan** Objective: Determine whether the Defense Logistics Agency Disposition Services is properly disposing of equipment during the drawdown in Afghanistan. Specifically, we will determine whether adequate controls exist over the receipt, inspection, coding, and disposal of equipment. (Project: D2013-D000JB-0129.000)	Apr-13	Dec-13	9
COPSWA Ref. No. 916 **Assessment of U.S. Government Efforts to Transition Security Cooperation and Assistance Activities Supporting the GIRoA From DoD Authority to DOS Authority** Objectives: Determine whether: (1) U.S. Government goals, objectives, plans, and guidance are sufficient, issued and operative for the transition of the CSTC-A security assistance activities in Afghanistan from DoD authority to a security cooperation organization under DOS authority and (2) ongoing efforts by U.S. forces to provide security assistance to the GIRoA are adversely impacted by the implementation of drawdown plans for U.S. Forces-Afghanistan and the transition of ISAF and International Security Assistance Force Joint Command to a command organization under authority. (Project: D2013-D00SPO-0181.000)	Jun-13	Apr-14	11
COPSWA Ref. No. 918 **ANA Metrics Product** Objective: Provide a summary of the ANA readiness to take the lead in Afghanistan security operations relative to U.S. forces withdrawal scheduled for 2014. (Project: D2011-D00SPO-0182.008)	Sep-13	Mar-14	1

Project	Start	Final	Strategic Issue
COPSWA Ref. No. 919 **Audit of the Transition of Facilities to the Logistics Civil Augmentation Program IV Density List at Kandahar Airfield, Afghanistan** Objective: Determine whether the DoD is properly monitoring the transition of newly constructed or remodeled facilities to the Logistics Civil Augmentation Program IV Density List at Kandahar Airfield, Afghanistan. (Project: D2013-D000JB-0050.000)	Nov-12	Sep-13	11
COPSWA Ref. No. 1042 **Price Reasonableness Determinations for Datron World Communications, Inc. Contracts Awarded by the U.S. Army Contracting Command for the ANSF** Objective: Determine whether the U.S. Army Contracting Command obtained fair and reasonable prices for communications equipment and components procured from Datron World Communications, Inc. for the ANSF. (Project: D2013-D000AT-0083.000)	Jan-13	Nov-13	1 10
COPSWA Ref. No. 1076 **Audit of the Security and Handling of Equipment Staged for Retrograde at Aerial Ports of Debarkation in Afghanistan** Objective: Determine whether DoD has effective controls over the storing and handling of equipment staged for shipment at the Aerial Ports of Debarkation in Afghanistan. (Project: D2013-D000JB-0149.000)	Apr-13	Dec-13	9
COPSWA Ref. No. 1170 **Ministry of Defense/General Staff/ANA Logistics Development** Objective: Evaluate progress made since previous assessments of this area, with a probable focus on execution or outcome of plans currently being developed by the CSTC-A Executive Director of ANSF Sustainment. (Project: SPO/TBD)	Oct-13	Jun-14	1
COPSWA Ref. No. 1171 **ANP Metrics Product** Objective: Provide a summary of ANP readiness to sustain the lead in Afghanistan security operations relative to U.S. forces withdrawal schedule for 2014. (Project: D2011-D00SPO-0182-009)	Dec-13	Jun-14	1
COPSWA Ref. No. 1172 **ANA Metrics Product** Objective: Provide a summary of ANA readiness to sustain the lead in Afghanistan security operations relative to U.S. forces withdrawal schedule for 2014. (Project: D2011-D00SPO-0181.010)	Mar-14	Sep-14	1

Project	Start	Final	Strategic Issue
COPSWA Ref. No. 1173 **Post-2014 ANSF Train and Equip** Objective: DoD OIG is continuing its oversight of the train and equip mission for Afghan Forces. A specific objective for this continuing series will be determined once the Department makes further decisions on post-2014 troop levels and missions. (Project: SPO/TBD)	Mar-14	Dec-14	1
COPSWA Ref. No. 1284 **Property Losses in Afghanistan** Objective: Determine whether DoD complied with applicable regulations for reporting equipment losses in Afghanistan and whether the losses have been accurately recorded in accountability systems. (Project: AUD/TBD)	Oct-13	Jun-14	9
COPSWA Ref. No. 1285 **Retrograde of Force Provider Equipment** Objective: Determine whether DoD is effectively retrograding force provider equipment from Afghanistan and whether the equipment is appropriately accounted for in its systems of record. (Project: AUD/TBD)	Oct-13	Jun-14	9
COPSWA Ref. No. 1286 **ANSF Mi-17, Mi-35, AN-26, and AN-32 Aircraft Spare Parts - Accountability** Objective: Determine whether U.S. Army officials properly planned, procured, stored, and maintained accountability of aircraft parts for the ANSF. We plan to conduct a series of audits to meet this objective. In the first audit, we will determine whether the Army properly accounted for and controlled parts inventories purchased to support the ANSF; and whether those parts were properly delivered to the ANSF. (Project: AUD/TBD)	Dec-13	Oct-14	10 11
COPSWA Ref. No. 1287 **Afghan Air Force Light Air Support Aircraft – Contract Administration** Objective: Determine whether U.S. Air Force officials properly awarded, administered, planned, and implemented the Light Air Support Indefinite-Delivery, Indefinite-Quantity contract. We plan to conduct a series of audits to meet this objective. In the first audit, we will determine whether Air Force officials properly awarded, administered, and planned the Light Air Support Indefinite-Delivery, Indefinite-Quantity contract. (Project: AUD/TBD)	Dec-13	Oct-14	10 11
COPSWA Ref. No. 1291 **Afghanistan Base Closure and Facilities Management** Objective: Determine whether DoD officials have adequately planned and executed the closure of U.S. bases in Afghanistan, including the status of completed and ongoing MILCON projects when retaining, transferring, or closing bases. (Project: AUD/TBD)	Apr-14	Dec-14	9 10

Project	Start	Final	Strategic Issue
COPSWA Ref. No. 1292 **Contracting Support in Afghanistan** Objective: Determine whether contracts to support U.S. forces in Afghanistan adequately describe the functions required and have proper oversight. (Project: AUD/TBD)	Apr-14	Dec-14	10
COPSWA Ref. No. 1321 **ANSF Mi-17, Mi-35, AN-26, and AN-32 Aircraft Spare Parts - Requirements** Objective: Determine whether the Army based the development of requirements for the ANSF aircraft spare parts on realistic and sustainable logistical plans. This is the second in a series of projects the DoD OIG plans to perform on ANSF aircraft spare parts. . (Project: AUD/TBD)	Mar-14	Jan-15	10 11
COPSWA Ref. No. 1322 **Afghan Air Force Light Air Support (LAS)Aircraft – Contract Oversight** Objective: This is the second in a series of projects the DoD OIG plans to perform on ANSF aircraft spare parts. DoD OIG will determine whether Air Force officials effectively implemented oversight of the LAS Aircraft. (Project: AUD/TBD)	Mar-14	Jan-15	10 11

U.S. Army Audit Agency

Project	Start	Final	Strategic Issue
COPSWA Ref. No. 882 **LOGCAP IV-Managing Drawdown** Objectives: (1) Verify that adjustments to requirements during the drawdown are economical and synchronized with base closures. (2) Verify that contracts are appropriately incentivized to manage contract drawdown. (Project: A-2012-MTE-0424.000)	Aug-12	Nov-13	10
COPSWA Ref. No. 923 **Retrograde of Class V in Afghanistan** Objectives: (1) Verify that asset visibility and accountability is accurately established and maintained throughout movement to the final destination. (2) Verify that asset disposition decisions are economical and represent the best value to the Army. (Project: A-2013-MTE-0139.000)	Dec-12	Sep-13	9
COPSWA Ref. No. 1034 **Force Protection-Base Access Controls** Objectives: (1) Verify that processes and procedures for issuing and tracking base access badges effectively limit base access to authorized personnel. (2) Verify that processes and procedures for validating and monitoring vehicle and equipment movements on and off base limit movements to authorized missions. (Project: A-2013-MTE-0135.000)	Jan-13	Oct-13	8
COPSWA Ref. No. 1035 **Force Protection-Contractor Accountability** Objective: Verify that processes and procedures for vetting, tracking and accounting for contractor personnel (prime/subcontractor) provided the visibility to ensure personnel had appropriate privileges and clearances. (Project: A-2013-MTE-0138.000)	Nov-12	Sep-13	10
COPSWA Ref. No. 1036 **Management of Materiel Handling Equipment** Objectives: (1) Verify that requirements for materiel handling equipment are effectively managed in line with theater drawdown strategies. (2) Verify that materiel handling equipment supporting Army operations are effectively utilized. (3) Verify that the acquisition strategy for materiel handling equipment used to support operations on enduring Afghanistan bases is cost effective. (Project: A-2013-MTE-0137.000)	Jan-13	Nov-13	9

Project	Start	Final	Strategic Issue
COPSWA Ref. No. 1078 **Repatriating Loaned Equipment** Objectives: Verify that processes and procedures for: (1) repatriating equipment loaned to coalition partners resulted in the return of equipment in the appropriate configuration and condition and (2) initiating and processing (when required) financial liability investigation of property loss actions for equipment loaned to coalition partners resulted in appropriate resolution. (Project: A-2013-MTE-0241.000)	Aug-13	Feb-14	9
COPSWA Ref. No. 1079 **Contract Drawdown** Objective: Verify that processes and procedures for re-evaluating requirements and adjusting select contracts effectively kept the scope of contracts in line with the force structure. (Project: A-2013-MTE-0240.000)	Aug-13	Feb-14	10
COPSWA Ref. No. 1080 **Retrograde of Sensitive Equipment and Materiel** Objective: Verify that processes and procedures for packaging, shipping, and tracking sensitive materiel provide appropriate security/protection. (Project: TBD)	Jan-14	Jun-14	9
COPSWA Ref. No. 1081 **Surface Tender CENTCOM Region (STCR) Program** Objectives: Verify that the: (1) Surface Tender CENTCOM Region program has sufficient controls in place and operating to ensure compliance with financial and acquisition regulations, and strategic goals for financial transparency and good stewardship and (2) Surface Tender CENTCOM Region program has sufficient processes, procedures, and metrics in place and is operating to ensure best value is achieved, and program objectives and goals are met. (Project: A-2013-MTE-0239.000)	Aug-13	Feb-14	10
COPSWA Ref. No. 1131 **Linguist Contract Requirements** Objective: Verify that the Army has sufficient processes and procedures for identifying and validating requirements for Linguist Contracts in Southwest Asia. (Project: A-2013-FMI-0107.000)	Aug-13	Feb-14	10

Naval Audit Service

Project	Start	Final	Strategic Issue
COPSWA Ref. No. 168 **Marine Reserve Mobilization Orders** Objective: Verify that internal controls provide reasonable assurance that Marine Corps Reserve CONUS mobilization orders are properly authorized, performed, and paid in accordance with applicable directives. (Project: N2011-NMC000-0105.000)	Jul-11	Sep-13	11
COPSWA Ref. No. 184 **Navy Individual Augmentee (IA) Reintegration Process** Objective: Verify that Navy Individual Augmentees are provided the intended support throughout the deployment cycle to reintegrate with family, community, and employers. (Project: 2012-070)	Dec-11	Oct-13	11

U.S. Air Force Audit Agency

Project	Start	Final	Strategic Issue
COPSWA Ref. No. 896 **Remote Piloted Aircraft Maintenance and Accountability** Objective: Evaluate whether the Air Force effectively managed remote piloted aircraft. Specifically, assess whether personnel developed and maintained unit type codes addressing current mission needs, timely accomplished maintenance actions, and properly accounted for assets. (Project: F2012-O30000-0846)	Jul-12	Sep-13	9
COPSWA Ref. No. 931 **Afghanistan Base Closure Plans** Objective: Evaluate base closure plans for Afghanistan. Specifically, determine whether U.S. Air Forces Central Command (AFCENT) (1) develops complete and accurate base closure plans for a timely and organized redeployment from Afghanistan and (2) effectively monitors base execution. (Project: F2013-O30000-0032)	Jul-13	Sep-14	9
COPSWA Ref. No. 932 **Patient Movement Items (PMI)** Objectives: Determine whether Air Force Medical Service officials effectively manage patient movement items. Specifically, determine whether medical officials properly: (1) establish and fund equipment requirements and (2) maintain and account for patient movement items. (Project: F2013-O40000-0042)	Oct-13	Sep-14	9
COPSWA Ref. No. 1077 **Mission Capability (MICAP) Parts** Objectives: Determine if Air Force Logistics personnel effectively managed mission capability parts. Specifically, determine if logistics personnel (1) properly supported and accurately documented mission capability parts requisitions and (2) properly processed and timely satisfied mission capability parts requirements. (Project: F2013-L40000-0533.000)	Mar-13	Sep-14	9
COPSWA Ref. No. 1189 **Follow-Up Audit, Pallets** Objective: Determine if management implemented corrective actions in response to AFAA Audit Report F2009-0006-FC4000, Feb 4, 2009. Specifically, determine if management implemented actions to accurately compute pallet requirements, maintain accurate pallet inventory data, and implement an effective retrograde program. (Project: F2013-L40000-0962.000)	Jul-13	Jul-14	9

Project	Start	Final	Strategic Issue
COPSWA Ref. No. 1190 **Air Force Equipment Management Systems (AFEMS) Accuracy** Objective: Determine if personnel effectively managed AFEMS data. Specifically, determine if logistics personnel accurately recorded item data, accurately accounted for equipment items in AFEMS, and consistently reported information between AFEMS and the Standard Base Supply System. (Project: TBD)	May-14	May-15	9
COPSWA Ref. No. 1191 **Wireless Network Security** Objective: Evaluate management of Second Generation Wireless Local Area network (2GWLAN) security in the AFCENT AOR. Specifically, determine whether Air Force officials effectively manage wireless network and device authorization, configuration, and operation. (Project: TBD)	May-14	May-15	9
COPSWA Ref. No. 1192 **Moral Network Operations** Objective: Determine whether Air Force Central Command personnel effectively and efficiently manage the Moral Network in deployed locations. Specifically, determine if management properly locates moral networks in authorized common areas, properly funds moral networks, and effectively performs contract administration when required. (Project: TBD)	May-14	May-15	9
COPSWA Ref. No. 1193 **Bulk Fuel Management** Objective: Evaluate bulk fuel management in the AFCENT Southwest Asia AOR. Specifically, determine whether the Air Force accurately accounts for fuel, pays appropriate fees, and properly maintains bulk fuel storage tanks in the AOR. (Project: TBD)	May-14	May-15	9
COPSWA Ref. No. 1194 **Follow-Up, AFCENT War Reserved Materiel (WRM)** Objective: Evaluate management corrective actions taken in response to report of audit F2009-0003-FD3000, AFCENT War Reserve Materiel. Specifically, determine if AFCENT accurately identifies War Reserve Materiel requirements and authorizations, and properly accounts for War Reserve Materiel assets. (Project: TBD)	Apr-14	May-15	9
COPSWA Ref. No. 1195 **Inter-Theater Airlift Supporting CENTCOM** Objective: Evaluate whether the Air Force effectively manages inter-theater airlift supporting CENTCOM. Specifically, determine if planners accurately plan and execute airlift configurations and load to maximize airlift capacity. (Project: TBD)	Feb-14	May-15	9

Special Inspector General for Afghanistan Reconstruction

Project	Start	Final	Strategic Issue
COPSWA Ref. No. 823 **Base Construction Requirements and Transition Procedures for ANSF** Objectives: Determine the extent to which (1) U.S. and coalition basing plans for the ANSF reflect ANSF force strength projections; (2) CSTC-A analyzed alternatives to minimize new construction, including using existing U.S. and coalition bases to satisfy ANSF basing needs; and (3) appropriate criteria have been developed and applied to ensure that current and proposed construction projects for the ANSF are necessary, achievable, and able to be sustained by the Afghan government. (Project: SIGAR-069A)	Sep-12	Sep-13	1
COPSWA Ref. No. 937 **USAID's Direct Assistance to the Afghan Ministry of Public Health (MoPH) for Public Hospitals** Objectives: Determine the extent to which (1) U.S. direct assistance to the Afghan Ministry of Public Health for public hospitals is used for intended purposes and delivering expected outcomes and (2) USAID and the Afghan Ministry of Public Health implemented the financial and other controls established in the bilateral direct assistance agreement. (Project: SIGAR-068A)	Aug-12	Sep-13	7
COPSWA Ref. No. 950 **ANP Logistics Capability for Petroleum, Oil, and Lubricants (POL)** Objectives: (1) Determine whether the budget requests submitted for ANP Petroleum, Oil, and Lubricants are reasonable considering actual fuel funding levels needed to meet ANP mission requirements. (2) Evaluate the internal controls in place to determine if they are sufficient to account for Petroleum, Oil, and Lubricants and to prevent fraud, waste, and abuse. (Project: SIGAR-070A)	Sep-12	Sep-13	1 5

Project	Start	Final	Strategic Issue
COPSWA Ref. No. 959 **Contracts for ANSF Literacy Training** Objectives: Determine whether (1) contract requirements for training were supported; (2) training was conducted by qualified contractor instructors in accordance with contract terms; (3) DoD officials measured and monitored training outcomes and took actions to address performance issues; and (4) payments to the contractor were based on services provided and were consistent with terms of the contract. (Project: SIGAR-072A)	Nov-12	Oct-13	1 7
COPSWA Ref. No. 966 **U.S. Training of Afghan Justice Sector Personnel** Objectives: Examine the implementation and oversight of U.S. efforts to train Afghan justice sector personnel to improve the capacity of Afghanistan's judicial system and overall rule of law. We plan to focus primarily on DOS Bureau of International Narcotics and Law Enforcement (INL) Justice Sector Support Program (JSSP). Specifically, (1) assess whether JSSP contractor(s) provided qualified trainers and services in accordance with the terms of the contract(s); (2) determine the extent to which State monitored and evaluate contractor performance and training outcomes; and (3) assess the extent to which State measures the JSSP's effectiveness in achieving U.S. goals of developing the capacity of Afghanistan's justice sector. In addition, we will describe DoD and USAID justice sector training efforts and determine the extent to which these programs complement the JSSP. (Project: SIGAR-073A)	Dec-12	Oct-13	2 7
COPSWA Ref. No. 967 **Rule of Law Programs-Outcomes and Sustainability** Objectives: (1) Determine the extent that rule-of-law programs are achieving their goals and objectives. (2) Determine the actions taken to reevaluate the strategic approach and direction of programs in response to performance metrics and outcomes achieved. (3) Determine whether rule-of-law programs have complied with the USAID Administrator's guidance on sustainability. (Project: TBD)	Nov-13	May-14	5

Project	Start	Final	Strategic Issue
COPSWA Ref. No. 1033 **DoD's Procurement and Management of Class IX (Automotive) Repair Parts for the ANSF** Objectives: Examine DoD's procurement and management of Class IX (automotive) repair parts for the ANSF. Specifically, we will (1) assess the process CSTC-A uses to determine requirements and to acquire, manage, store and distribute Class IX repair parts for the ANSF and (2) evaluate whether internal controls are sufficient to account for Class IX repair parts and prevent fraud, waste, and abuse. (Project: SIGAR-071A)	Oct-12	Oct-13	1
COPSWA Ref. No. 1056 **Evaluation of Progress Made in Meeting U.S. Anti-Corruption Goals in Afghanistan** Objectives: Evaluate progress made in meeting the U.S. anti-corruption strategy for Afghanistan and related goals and objectives. Specifically, SIGAR will: (1) identify the U.S. strategic goals and objectives for reducing corruption in Afghanistan and (2) assess progress made in achieving those stated goals and objectives against identified benchmarks and/or performance targets. (Project: SIGAR-SP-6)	Feb-13	Sep-13	5
COPSWA Ref. No. 1059 **Reliability of ANSF Personnel Data** Objectives: Examine ANSF personnel data reliability. Specifically, we will (1) assess the reliability and usefulness of data for the number of ANSF authorized, assigned, and trained and (2) review the methodology for gathering data on ANSF personnel, including the extent to which the DoD reviews and validates the information collected. (Project: SIGAR-079A)	Mar-13	Oct-13	1 7
COPSWA Ref. No. 1061 **Financial Audit of USAID Cooperative Agreement 306-A-00-09-00511-00 With Central Asia Development Group (CADG) for the Community Development Program (CDP)** Objective: Conduct a financial audit of costs incurred under the award for the period 03/12/2009 - 03/31/2013. (Project: SIGAR F-013)	Jun-13	Dec-13	7
COPSWA Ref. No. 1062 **Financial Audit of USAID Contracts 306-M-00-07-00502-00 and 306-DFD-I-04-00170-00 With Checchi and Company Consulting, Inc. for Results Tracking Services and Rule of Law Stabilization Program** Objective: Conduct a financial audit of costs incurred under the two contracts for the respective periods of 10/09/2006 - 08/27/2012 and 03/19/2010 - 08/31/2011. (Project: SIGAR F-014)	Jun-13	Dec-13	7

Project	Start	Final	Strategic Issue
COPSWA Ref. No. 1063 **Financial Audit of USAID Contract 306-M-00-06-00508-00 and Cooperative Agreement 306-A-00-10-00513-00 With Creative Associates International for the Building Education Support System for Teachers (BESST) and the Community Based Stabilization (CBSG) Programs** Objective: Conduct a financial audit of costs incurred under the contract and the cooperative agreement for the respective periods of 01/27/2006 - 08/31/2011 and 03/07/2010 - 03/06/2012. (Project: SIGAR F-015)	Jun-13	Dec-13	7
COPSWA Ref. No. 1064 **Financial Audit of USAID Cooperative Agreement 306-A-00-06-00523-00 With JHPIEGO Corp. for the Health Service Support Project (HSSP)** Objective: Conduct a financial audit of costs incurred under the cooperative agreement for the period 02/15/2005 - 06/30/2009. (Project: SIGAR F-016)	Jun-13	Dec-13	7
COPSWA Ref. No. 1065 **Financial Audit of USAID Cooperative Agreement 306-A-00-09-00512-00 With Mercy Corps for the Community Development Program (CDP) in Balkh, Kunduz, Baghlan, and Bamyan** Objective: Conduct a financial audit of costs incurred under the cooperative agreement for the period 03/10/2009 - 12/31/2011. (Project: SIGAR F-017)	Jun-13	Dec-13	7
COPSWA Ref. No. 1066 **Financial Audit of USAID Cooperative Agreement 306-A-00-09-00510-00 With CARE International for the CDP in Kabul** Objective: Conduct a financial audit of costs incurred under the cooperative agreement for the period 03/08/2009 - 11/30/2011. (Project: SIGAR F-018)	Jun-13	Dec-13	7
COPSWA Ref. No. 1067 **Financial Audit of USAID Contract 306-C-00-09-00531-00 With World Council of Credit Unions for the Rural Finance and Cooperative Development (RUFCOD) Program** Objective: Conduct a financial audit of costs incurred under the contract for the period 12/06/2009 - 12/05/2011. (Project: SIGAR F-019)	Jun-13	Dec-13	7
COPSWA Ref. No. 1068 **Financial Audit of USAID Cooperative Agreement 306-A-00-05-00511-00 With Counterpart International, Inc. for the Initiative to Promote Afghan Civil Society (IPACS I) Program** Objective: Conduct a financial audit of costs incurred under the cooperative agreement for the period 01/03/2005 - 09/30/2010. (Project: SIGAR F-020)	Jun-13	Dec-13	7

Project	Start	Final	Strategic Issue
COPSWA Ref. No. 1069 **Financial Audit of USAID Contract 306-EPP-I-11-03-00006-00** **With International Resources Group for the Afghan Clean Energy** **Program (ACEP)** Objective: Conduct a financial audit of costs incurred under the contract for the period 09/09/2009 - 01/31/2012. (Project: SIGAR F-032)	Jun-13	Dec-13	7
COPSWA Ref. No. 1070 **Financial Audit of USAID Cooperative Agreement** **306-A-00-09-00513-00 With World Vision for the CDP in Herat,** **Qala-i-Naw, Chaghcharan** Objective: Conduct a financial audit of costs incurred under the cooperative agreement for the period 03/11/2009 - 01/15/2011. (Project: SIGAR F-021)	Jun-13	Dec-13	7
COPSWA Ref. No. 1071 **Financial Audit of Various Department of State Grants to Afghan** **Technical Consultants for the Removal of Land Mines and** **Unexploded Ordnance** Objective: Conduct a financial audit of costs incurred under the grants for the period 04/01/2007 - 03/31/2012. (Project: SIGAR F-022)	Jun-13	Dec-13	7
COPSWA Ref. No. 1074 **USAID Assistance to Afghanistan's Water Sector** Objectives: Examine the extent to which USAID has assisted Afghanistan's water sector since FY 2010 and the outcomes of those efforts. Specifically, we will evaluate the extent to which: (1) completed, ongoing, and planned projects meet USAID's project goals and objectives and align with the 2010 U.S. Interagency Water Strategy for Afghanistan and (2) plans incorporate sustainability within ongoing and planned water projects. (Project: SIGAR-077A)	Mar-13	Oct-13	3

Project	Start	Final	Strategic Issue
COPSWA Ref. No. 1075 **U.S. Government Reconstruction Transition Plan** Objectives: Determine the extent to which the U.S. Government has developed plans for transitioning reconstruction projects and assets in Afghanistan. Specifically, we plan to: (1) Determine the extent to which U.S. Government agencies involved in Afghanistan reconstruction have transition plans in place and how those plans fit into the overall U.S. Government strategy. (2) Evaluate the extent to which transition plans include guidance on the asset transfer process and clarification on roles and responsibilities. (3) Assess whether a comprehensive inventory of ongoing and completed U.S. reconstruction projects and assets has been developed and documented, including those projects and assets already turned over to the Afghan government. (4) Determine the progress made in obtaining Afghan government support for a formal asset-transfer agreement, including the extent to which the Afghan government has developed plans to support U.S.-transferred projects and assets. (5) Identify how U.S. agencies plan to address any limitations in the Afghan government's capacity to maintain reconstruction projects and assets. (Project: SIGAR-080A)	Apr-13	Nov-13	2 11
COPSWA Ref. No. 1082 **Afghan Ministries of Defense (MOD) and Interior Affairs Capacity Assessments** Objectives: (1) Review the findings of DoD's assessments of Ministry of Interior and MOD's capacity to manage and account for direct assistance. (2) Assess how DoD intends to use these assessments when making decisions about providing direct assistance to MOD and Ministry of Interior and how DoD intends to mitigate financial management and internal controls challenges at Ministry of Interior and MOD. (Project: SIGAR SP-12)	Apr-13	Sep-13	6
COPSWA Ref. No. 1085 **Inspections of Medical, Education, and Police Facilities in Kabul Province (Gardez Hospital)** Objectives: Determine whether (1) construction was completed, or is being done, in accordance with contract requirements and applicable construction standards; (2) construction deficiencies are being corrected before acceptance and transfer; and (3) facilities are being used as intended and maintained. (Project: SIGAR-I-005A)	Sep-12	Oct-13	3 7

Project	Start	Final	Strategic Issue
COPSWA Ref. No. 1087 **Inspections of Medical, Education, and Police Facilities in Kabul Province (Veayer Ahmad School)** Objectives: Determine whether (1) construction was completed, or is being done, in accordance with contract requirements and applicable construction standards; (2) construction deficiencies are being corrected before acceptance and transfer; and (3) facilities are being used as intended and maintained. (Project: SIGAR-I-005C)	Sep-12	Sep-14	3 7
COPSWA Ref. No. 1090 **Inspections of Medical, Education, and Police Facilities in Kabul Province (Walayatti Clinic)** Objectives: Determine whether (1) construction was completed, or is being done, in accordance with contract requirements and applicable construction standards; (2) construction deficiencies are being corrected before acceptance and transfer; and (3) facilities are being used as intended and maintained. (Project: SIGAR-I-005F)	Sep-12	Oct-13	3 7
COPSWA Ref. No. 1091 **Inspections of Medical, Education, and Police Facilities in Kabul Province (Paghman Clinic)** Objectives: Determine whether (1) construction was completed, or is being done, in accordance with contract requirements and applicable construction standards; (2) construction deficiencies are being corrected before acceptance and transfer; and (3) facilities are being used as intended and maintained. (Project: SIGAR-I-005H)	Sep-12	Oct-14	3 7
COPSWA Ref. No. 1092 **Inspections of Medical, Education, and Police Facilities in Kabul Province (AOB SOF Clinic)** Objectives: Determine whether (1) construction was completed, or is being done, in accordance with contract requirements and applicable construction standards; (2) construction deficiencies are being corrected before acceptance and transfer; and (3) facilities are being used as intended and maintained. (Project: SIGAR-I-005I)	Sep-12	Dec-15	3 7
COPSWA Ref. No. 1093 **Inspection of the Deh-e Sabz Slaughterhouse in Kabul Province** Objectives: Determine whether (1) construction was completed, or is being done, in accordance with contract requirements and applicable construction standards; (2) construction deficiencies are being corrected before acceptance and transfer; and (3) facilities are being used as intended and maintained. (Project: SIGAR-I-005J)	Sep-12	Dec-15	3 7

Project	Start	Final	Strategic Issue
COPSWA Ref. No. 1094 **Inspections of Medical, Education, and Police Facilities in Kabul Province (Ministry of Defense Headquarters)** Objectives: Determine whether (1) construction was completed, or is being done, in accordance with contract requirements and applicable construction standards; (2) construction deficiencies are being corrected before acceptance and transfer; and (3) facilities are being used as intended and maintained. (Project: SIGAR-I-005K)	Sep-12	Dec-15	3 7
COPSWA Ref. No. 1095 **Inspections of Medical, Education, and Police Facilities in the Northern Provinces (Archi District Police HQ)** Objectives: Focus on medical, education, and police facilities in the Northern Provinces. Specifically, we will determine whether (1) construction was completed, or is being done, in accordance with contract requirements and applicable construction standards; (2) construction deficiencies are corrected before acceptance and transfer; and (3) facilities are used as intended and maintained. (Project: SIGAR-I-006B)	Sep-12	Oct-13	3 7
COPSWA Ref. No. 1103 **Inspections of Medical, Education, and Police Facilities in the Northern Provinces (3rd Kandak Monitor)** Objectives: Focus on medical, education, and police facilities in the Northern Provinces. Specifically, we will determine whether (1) construction was completed, or is being done, in accordance with contract requirements and applicable construction standards; (2) construction deficiencies are corrected before acceptance and transfer; and (3) facilities are used as intended and maintained. (Project: SIGAR-I-006L)	Sept-12	Nov-13	3 7
COPSWA Ref. No. 1107 **Inspections of Medical, Education, and Police Facilities in the Northern Provinces (TTF MeS)** Objectives: Focus on medical, education, and police facilities in the Northern Provinces. Specifically, we will determine whether (1) construction was completed, or is being done, in accordance with contract requirements and applicable construction standards; (2) construction deficiencies are corrected before acceptance and transfer; and (3) facilities are used as intended and maintained. (Project: SIGAR-I-006P)	Sep-12	Nov-13	3 7

Project	Start	Final	Strategic Issue
COPSWA Ref. No. 1109 **Inspections of Medical, Education, and Police Facilities in the Northern Provinces (UP Prov. HQ Pole Khumri)** Objectives: Focus on medical, education, and police facilities in the Northern Provinces. Specifically, we will determine whether (1) construction was completed, or is being done, in accordance with contract requirements and applicable construction standards; (2) construction deficiencies are corrected before acceptance and transfer; and (3) facilities are used as intended and maintained. (Project: SIGAR-I-006R)	Sep-12	Oct-14	3 7
COPSWA Ref. No. 1110 **Inspections of Medical, Education, and Police Facilities in the Northern Provinces (UP Dist. HQ Pole Khumri)** Objectives: Focus on medical, education, and police facilities in the Northern Provinces. Specifically, we will determine whether (1) construction was completed, or is being done, in accordance with contract requirements and applicable construction standards; (2) construction deficiencies are corrected before acceptance and transfer; and (3) facilities are used as intended and maintained. (Project: SIGAR-I-006S)	Sep-12	Jun-14	3 7
COPSWA Ref. No. 1111 **Inspections of Medical, Education, and Police Facilities in the Northern Provinces (Provincial Response Co.)** Objectives: Focus on medical, education, and police facilities in the Northern Provinces. Specifically, we will determine whether (1) construction was completed, or is being done, in accordance with contract requirements and applicable construction standards; (2) construction deficiencies are corrected before acceptance and transfer; and (3) facilities are used as intended and maintained. (Project: SIGAR-I-006T)	Sep-12	Oct-14	3 7
COPSWA Ref. No. 1112 **Inspections of Medical, Education, and Police Facilities in the Northern Provinces (ANCOP Patrol BN)** Objectives: Focus on medical, education, and police facilities in the Northern Provinces. Specifically, we will determine whether (1) construction was completed, or is being done, in accordance with contract requirements and applicable construction standards; (2) construction deficiencies are corrected before acceptance and transfer; and (3) facilities are used as intended and maintained. (Project: SIGAR-I-006U)	Sep-12	Sep-14	3 7

Project	Start	Final	Strategic Issue
COPSWA Ref. No. 1116 **Inspections of Incinerators (Ghazni)** Objectives: Determine whether (1) a needs assessment for the incinerator was performed before construction, in order to determine base requirements and capacity needs; (2) construction was completed in accordance with contract requirements; (3) construction deficiencies are corrected before acceptance and transfer; and (4) incinerators are in use as intended. (Project: SIGAR I-007B)	Oct-12	Jan-14	3
COPSWA Ref. No. 1117 **Inspections of Incinerators (Shank)** Objectives: Determine whether (1) a needs assessment for the incinerator was performed before construction to determine base requirements and capacity needs; (2) construction was completed in accordance with contract requirements; (3) construction deficiencies are corrected before acceptance and transfer; and (4) incinerators are in use as intended. (Project: SIGAR I-007C)	Oct-12	Jan-14	3
COPSWA Ref. No. 1118 **Inspections of Incinerators (Sharana)** Objectives: Determine whether (1) a needs assessment for the incinerator was performed before construction to determine base requirements and capacity needs; (2) construction was completed in accordance with contract requirements; (3) construction deficiencies are corrected before acceptance and transfer; and (4) incinerators are in use as intended. (Project: SIGAR I-007D)	Oct-12	Oct-13	3
COPSWA Ref. No. 1119 **Inspections of Incinerators (Bagram)** Objectives: Determine whether (1) a needs assessment for the incinerator was performed before construction to determine base requirements and capacity needs; (2) construction was completed in accordance with contract requirements; (3) construction deficiencies are corrected before acceptance and transfer; and (4) incinerators are in use as intended. (Project: SIGAR I-007E)	Oct-12	Jan-14	3
COPSWA Ref. No. 1120 **Inspections of Incinerators (Kandahar)** Objectives: Determine whether (1) a needs assessment for the incinerator was performed before construction to determine base requirements and capacity needs; (2) construction was completed in accordance with contract requirements; (3) construction deficiencies are corrected before acceptance and transfer; and (4) incinerators are in use as intended. (Project: SIGAR I-007F)	Oct-12	Jan-14	3

Project	Start	Final	Strategic Issue
COPSWA Ref. No. 1122 **Inspections of Medical, Education, Police, and Agricultural Facilities in the Western Provinces** Objectives: Focus on medical, education, police, and agricultural facilities in the western provinces. Specifically, we will determine whether (1) construction was completed, or is being done, in accordance with contract requirements and applicable construction standards; (2) construction deficiencies are corrected before acceptance and transfer; and (3) facilities are used as intended and maintained and appropriately sustained. (Project: SIGAR-I-008A)	Feb-13	Mar-14	3 7
COPSWA Ref. No. 1123 **Inspections of Medical, Education, Police, and Agricultural Facilities in the Western Provinces** Objectives: Focus on medical, education, police, and agricultural facilities in the western provinces. Specifically, we will determine whether (1) construction was completed, or is being done, in accordance with contract requirements and applicable construction standards; (2) construction deficiencies are corrected before acceptance and transfer; and (3) facilities are used as intended and maintained and appropriately sustained. (Project: SIGAR-I-008B)	Feb-13	Jun-14	3 7
COPSWA Ref. No. 1124 **Inspections of Medical, Education, Police, and Agricultural Facilities in the Western Provinces** Objectives: Focus on medical, education, police, and agricultural facilities in the western provinces. Specifically, we will determine whether (1) construction was completed, or is being done, in accordance with contract requirements and applicable construction standards; (2) construction deficiencies are corrected before acceptance and transfer; and (3) facilities are used as intended and maintained and appropriately sustained. (Project: SIGAR-I-008C)	Feb-13	Mar-15	3 7
COPSWA Ref. No. 1125 **Inspections of Medical, Education, Police, and Agricultural Facilities in the Western Provinces** Objectives: Focus on medical, education, police, and agricultural facilities in the western provinces. Specifically, we will determine whether (1) construction was completed, or is being done, in accordance with contract requirements and applicable construction standards; (2) construction deficiencies are corrected before acceptance and transfer; and (3) facilities are used as intended and maintained and appropriately sustained. (Project: SIGAR-I-008D)	Feb-13	Mar-15	3 7

Project	Start	Final	Strategic Issue
COPSWA Ref. No. 1126 **Inspection of the Kajaki Dam and Related Construction Projects in Helmand Province (1 of 4 inspections)** Objectives: Focus on the Kajaki Dam and related construction projects in Helmand Province including, but not limited, to USACE and USAID projects. Specifically, we will determine whether: (1) construction was completed, or is being done, in accordance with contract requirements and applicable construction standards; (2) construction deficiencies are corrected before acceptance and transfer; and (3) facilities are used as intended and maintained and appropriately sustained. (Project: SIGAR-I-009A)	Feb-13	Mar-14	3 7
COPSWA Ref. No. 1127 **Inspection of the Kajaki Dam and Related Construction Projects in Helmand Province (2 of 4 inspections)** Objectives: Focus on the Kajaki Dam and related construction projects in Helmand Province including, but not limited, to USACE and USAID projects. Specifically, we will determine whether: (1) construction was completed, or is being done, in accordance with contract requirements and applicable construction standards; (2) construction deficiencies are corrected before acceptance and transfer; and (3) facilities are used as intended and maintained and appropriately sustained. (Project: SIGAR-I-009B)	Feb-13	Jun-14	3 7
COPSWA Ref. No. 1128 **Inspection of the Kajaki Dam and Related Construction Projects in Helmand Province (3 of 4 inspections)** Objectives: Focus on the Kajaki Dam and related construction projects in Helmand Province including, but not limited, to USACE and USAID projects. Specifically, we will determine whether: (1) construction was completed, or is being done, in accordance with contract requirements and applicable construction standards; (2) construction deficiencies are corrected before acceptance and transfer; and (3) facilities are used as intended and maintained and appropriately sustained. (Project: SIGAR-I-009C)	Feb-13	Mar-15	3 7
COPSWA Ref. No. 1129 **Inspection of the Kajaki Dam and Related Construction Projects in Helmand Province (4 of 4 inspections)** Objectives: Focus on the Kajaki Dam and related construction projects in Helmand Province including, but not limited, to USACE and USAID projects. Specifically, we will determine whether: (1) construction was completed, or is being done, in accordance with contract requirements and applicable construction standards; (2) construction deficiencies are corrected before acceptance and transfer; and (3) facilities are used as intended and maintained and appropriately sustained. (Project: SIGAR-I-009D)	Feb-13	Mar-15	3 7

Project	Start	Final	Strategic Issue
COPSWA Ref. No. 1130 **Assessments of Afghan Ministerial Capacity** Objectives: Focus on USAID's efforts to assess the ability of GIRoA to manage and account for funds provided through direct or "on budget" assistance. SIGAR will describe the purpose of the assessments, summarize the findings of the assessments, and assess how USAID is using and plans to use the results of these assessments, particularly in the context of providing direct or "on budget" assistance to GIRoA. (Project: SIGAR-A-081A)	Apr-13	Oct-13	2 6
COPSWA Ref. No. 1136 **Financial Audit of Costs Incurred Under Cooperative Agreement 306-A-00-08-00509-00 With International Relief and Development, Inc. the Strategic Provincial Roads – Southern and Eastern Afghanistan Project** Objective: Conduct a financial audit of costs incurred under the contract for the period 11/30/2007 - 12/31/2012. (Project: SIGAR-F-012)	Feb-13	Oct-13	7
COPSWA Ref. No. 1137 **U.S. Efforts to Develop and Strengthen the Capacity of Afghanistan's Central Bank (DABS)** Objectives: Evaluate: (1) the steps taken by various U.S. agencies to strengthen the oversight and regulatory capacity of DAB after the near collapse of Kabul Bank and (2) the process that U.S. agencies use to provide direct assistance funds to Afghan ministries and the safeguards established to protect these funds from misuse while deposited in Afghan banks. (Project: SIGAR-082A)	Jun-13	Feb-14	2 6
COPSWA Ref. No. 1138 **Accountability of Weapons and Equipment Provided to the ANSF** Objectives: Evaluate (1) the procedures for the accountability of defense materiel and weapons procured by DoD to arm the ANSF and (2) the visibility and controls in place for the oversight of defense materials and weapons after being provided to the ANSF. (Project: SIGAR-A-078A)	Jun-13	Jan-14	1 7
COPSWA Ref. No. 1157 **Direct Assistance to the Da Afghanistan Breshna Sherkat (DABS) for the Kajaki Dam Project** Objectives: (1) Examine USAID's plans for providing direct assistance to Da Afghanistan Breshna Sherkat for Kajaki Dam. (2) Analyze USAID's assessment of Da Afghanistan Breshna Sherkat's capacity to manage direct assistance provided for the Kajaki Dam project and USAID's response to identified weaknesses. (3) Assess the measures, if any that USAID put in place to support Da Afghanistan Breshna Sherkat's ability to manage direct assistance, focused on those measures related to Kajaki Dam. (Project: SIGAR-SP-10)	Apr-13	Sep-13	6

Project	Start	Final	Strategic Issue
COPSWA Ref. No. 1158 **Inspection of the Justice Center in Parwan (JCIP) Court House Construction Project in Regional Command East, Afghanistan** Objectives: (1) Assess the proposal process and approval method by which the contractor was selected for the project; (2) determine whether construction was completed, or is being done, in accordance with contract requirements and applicable construction standards; and (3) discuss the current status of the project. (Project: SIGAR-I-010)	Jul-13	Oct-13	3 7
COPSWA Ref. No. 1160 **Efforts to Increase Afghanistan's Capacity to Assess and Collect Customs Revenue** Objectives: Evaluate the extent to which USAID and Department of Homeland Security Customs and Border Protection (CBP) (1) programs designed to reform Afghanistan's customs processes, procedures, and laws achieved intended outcomes and (2) programs designed to assist the Afghan government to generate customs revenues contributed to the fiscal sustainability of the Afghan government. (Project: SIGAR-083A)	Jul-13	Feb-14	2
COPSWA Ref. No. 1164 **Financial Audit of USAID Contracts 306-C-00-07-00503-00 and 306-DOT-I-02-08-00035-00 With Development Alternatives, Inc. for the Afghanistan Small and Medium Enterprise Development & Afghanistan Stabilization Initiative Programs** Objective: Conduct a financial audit of costs incurred under the contracts for the periods 10/26/2006 - 11/30/2012 and 11/1/2011 - 09/25/2012. (Project: SIGAR-F-023)	Sep-13	Mar-14	7
COPSWA Ref. No. 1165 **Financial Audit of USAID Contracts 306-DOT-I-01-08-00033-00 and 306-C-00-07-00501-00 With Chemonics International, Inc. for the Afghanistan Stabilization Initiative & Accelerated Sustainable Agriculture Programs** Objective: Conduct a financial audit of costs incurred under the contracts for the periods 06/26/2009 - 06/25/2012 and 11/22/2006 - 10/30/2011. (Project: SIGAR-F-024)	Sep-13	Mar-14	7
COPSWA Ref. No. 1177 **Mobile Strike Force Vehicles for the ANA** Objectives: (1) Evaluate the effectiveness of U.S. Government oversight of contracts to procure, operate, and maintain MSFVs for the ANA; and (2) determine the extent to which the ANA has the capacity to operate and maintain its current and planned MSFVs. (Project: SIGAR-085A)	Jul-13	Jan-14	1

Project	Start	Final	Strategic Issue
COPSWA Ref. No. 1283 **DoD's Use of Wire Transfers** Objectives: (1) Determine the amount of wire transfer fees that DoD, or other U.S. Government entities on behalf of DoD, paid between January 1, 2010, and January 1, 2013; and (2) determine the extent to which those fees are appropriate and reasonable based on applicable law, contracts, regulations, and standards. (Project: SIGAR-084A)	Jul-13	Feb-14	2
COPSWA Ref. No. 1290 **Audit of Afghan Women's Initiatives Funded by the** **U.S. Government** Objectives: (1) Identify U.S. Government programs or initiatives to improve the rights and treatment of women in Afghanistan since FY 2011; (2) assess the extent to which these programs and initiatives have been coordinated across different U.S. Government agencies; and (3) identify challenges in addressing women's issues in Afghanistan and evaluate U.S. efforts to address these challenges. (Project: SIGAR-087A)	Aug-13	Mar-14	3
COPSWA Ref. No. 1293 **Review of Education Projects in Afghanistan** Objectives: (1) Identify the objectives of U.S. Government projects and programs which expand access to and improve the quality of education; assess the extent to which metrics are capturing the progress of those projects; and evaluate the extent to which completed and ongoing projects have achieved or are achieving stated objectives. (2) Assess the transition from completed education projects to recently awarded or planned projects, and the extent to which planned projects consider lessons learned. (3) Evaluate the level of coordination among U.S. agencies involved in improving the education sector and the extent to which projects implemented by those agencies contribute to the goal of a healthy workforce with relevant skills and knowledge. (Project: SIGAR-086A)	Jul-13	Mar-14	2
COPSWA Ref. No. 1295 **Review of Equipment Provided to the Afghan Air Force Through the FY 2014 ASFF** Objectives: Evaluate the extent to which the AAF has the personnel with the technical expertise required to operate, maintain, and sustain the additional $1.07 billion in new air assets contained in the FY 2014 ASFF budget. (Project: TBD)	Oct-13	Jan-14	1

Project	Start	Final	Strategic Issue
COPSWA Ref. No. 1297 **Effectiveness of U.S. Counternarcotics Programs** Objectives: (1) Assess the effectiveness of the current counternarcotics strategy and programs; (2) assess U.S. agencies' monitoring and evaluation of counternarcotics programs; (3) evaluate the extent to which various U.S. agencies working on counternarcotics coordinate their efforts; and (4) assess the extent to which the Afghan government is prepared to sustain counternarcotics programs after 2014. (Project: TBD)	Dec-13	Jun-14	4
COPSWA Ref. No. 1298 **Review of Cash and Local Payments for ANSF Fuel** Objectives: (1) Evaluate the extent to which CSTC-A uses local finance offices (including cash and check) to pay for fuel and (2) evaluate CSTC-A's internal controls to track payments and to what extent did CSTC-A follow these internal controls. (Project: TBD)	Oct-13	Feb-14	1
COPSWA Ref. No. 1299 **USAID Afghanistan Municipal Programs** Objectives: Evaluate the extent to which the USAID's Afghanistan municipal programs are accomplishing their goals to increase the capacity of municipalities, improve the delivery of municipal services to citizens, increase revenue generation, and increase citizen satisfaction and trust in targeted municipalities. Audit will examine Regional Afghanistan Municipality Program for Urban Populations (RAMP) in the North, East, and West and the Kabul City Initiative Program. (Project: TBD)	Dec-13	Jun-14	2
COPSWA Ref. No. 1300 **USAID Afghan Info Database** Objectives: (1) Determine and evaluate the effectiveness of the internal controls that ensure information in Afghan Info is accurate, timely, and consistent. (2) Evaluate the extent that information USAID provides to policymakers and stakeholders using this database is accurate, timely, and consistent. (Project: TBD)	Jan-14	Jul-14	7
COPSWA Ref. No. 1301 **USAID's Measuring Impact of Stabilization Initiative (MISTI)** Objectives: (1) Evaluate the extent to which USAID integrates Measuring Impact of Stabilization Initiative findings/approaches into the planning, implementation, and oversight of applicable projects and (2) determine the extent to which Measuring Impact of Stabilization Initiative has contributed to the wider community of practice on best practices and lessons learned. (Project: TBD)	Feb-14	Aug-14	7

Project	Start	Final	Strategic Issue
COPSWA Ref. No. 1302 **Afghanistan Telecommunications** Objectives: (1) Identify U.S. Government-funded efforts to assist the Afghan government in development/improvement of the telecommunications sector. (2) Evaluate the measurement of outcomes and the effectiveness of these efforts. (Project: TBD)	Feb-14	Aug-14	2
COPSWA Ref. No. 1303 **National Solidarity Program III (NSP)** Objectives: (1) To what extent does the National Solidarity Program III reinforce the social compact between state and citizen given, (2) the role of facilitating partners, and (3) the changes included in the High Risk Areas Implementation Strategy? To what extent has the National Solidarity Program III changed its operating method to be in support of the Afghanistan Peace and Reintegration Program? (Project: TBD)	Apr-14	Oct-14	2
COPSWA Ref. No. 1304 **Use of Third-Party Monitoring by USAID** Objectives: (1) Determine the extent and effectiveness of USAID's use of third-party monitoring to gather data on project status and contractor performance and (2) assess the extent to which USAID reviews, validates, and uses the information collected. (Project: TBD)	Apr-14	Oct-14	7
COPSWA Ref. No. 1316 **Inspections of Medical, Education, and Police Facilities in Kabul Province (Camp Commando)** Objectives: Determine whether (1) construction was completed, or is being done, in accordance with contract requirements and applicable construction standards; (2) construction deficiencies are being corrected before acceptance and transfer; and (3) facilities are being used as intended and maintained. (Project: SIGAR-I-005L)	Sep-12	Jan-14	3 7
COPSWA Ref. No. 1327 **Financial Audit of USAID Contract 306-DFD-A-00-00304-00 With International Relief and Development for the Afghanistan Vouchers for Increased Production in Agriculture Program** Objective: Conduct a financial audit of costs incurred under the contracts. (Project: SIGAR-F-025)	Nov-13	May-14	7
COPSWA Ref. No. 1328 **Financial Audit of USAID Contract No EPP-I-05-04-00019-00 With ARD, Inc. for the Sustainable Water Supply and Sanitation Project** Objective: Conduct a financial audit of costs incurred under the contracts. (Project: SIGAR-F-026)	Nov-13	May-14	7

Project	Start	Final	Strategic Issue
COPSWA Ref. No. 1329 **Financial Audit of USAID Contract 306-A-00-06-00519-00 With PACT for Media Development in Afghanistan** Objective: Conduct a financial audit of costs incurred under the contracts. (Project: SIGAR-F-027)	Nov-13	May-14	7
COPSWA Ref. No. 1330 **Financial Audit of USAID Contract 306-DFD-I-03-05-00125-00 AECOM for the Afghanistan Social Outreach Program** Objective: Conduct a financial audit of costs incurred under the contracts. (Project: SIGAR-F-028)	Nov-13	May-14	7
COPSWA Ref. No. 1331 **Financial Audit of USAID Contract 306-A-00-06-00518-00 With CARE USA for the Partnership for Advancing Community Based Education in Afghanistan** Objective: Conduct a financial audit of costs incurred under the contracts. (Project: SIGAR-F-029)	Nov-13	May-14	7
COPSWA Ref. No. 1332 **Financial Audit of USAID Contract 306-DFD-I-09-04-00173-00 With Tetra Tech DPK for Rule of Law Stabilization Program Formal Local Governance Program** Objective: Conduct a financial audit of costs incurred under the contracts. (Project: SIGAR-F-030)	Dec-13	Jun-14	7
COPSWA Ref. No. 1333 **Financial Audit of USAID Contract 306-A-00-07-00514-00 With International City Managers Association for the Afghanistan Municipal Strengthening Program** Objective: Conduct a financial audit of costs incurred under the contracts. (Project: SIGAR-F-031)	Dec-13	Jun-14	7
COPSWA Ref. No. 1334 **Financial Audit USAID Contract 306-EPP-I-11-03-00006-00 With International Resources Group for the Afghan Clean Energy Program** Objective: Conduct a financial audit of costs incurred under the contracts. (Project: SIGAR-F-032)	Dec-13	Jun-14	7
COPSWA Ref. No. 1335 **Financial Audit of DOS INL Contract SAQMPD05F2737 With Pacific Architects & Engineers (PAE) for the Afghan Clean Energy Program** Objective: Conduct a financial audit of costs incurred under the contracts. (Project: SIGAR-F-033)	Dec-13	Jun-14	7

Project	Start	Final	Strategic Issue
COPSWA Ref. No. 1336 **Financial Audit of Various Department of State Instruments With the Mine Clearance Planning Agency for Humanitarian Mine and Unexploded Ordnance (UXO) Clearance** Objective: Conduct a financial audit of costs incurred under the contracts. (Project: SIGAR-F-034)	Dec-13	Jun-14	7
COPSWA Ref. No. 1337 **Financial Audit of DOS PAS Contracts SAF20010CA014 and SAF20011GR142 With CETENA Group for Public Diplomacy** Objective: Conduct a financial audit of costs incurred under the contracts. (Project: SIGAR-F-035)	Dec-13	Jun-14	7
COPSWA Ref. No. 1338 **Financial Audit of DOS PAS Contract SAF20011CA026 With Sayed Majidi Architecture and Design (SMAD) for Public Diplomacy** Objective: Conduct a financial audit of costs incurred under the contracts. (Project: SIGAR-F-036)	Dec-13	Jun-14	7

Department of State Office of Inspector General

Project	Start	Final	Strategic Issue
COPSWA Ref. No. 545 **Audit of Bureau of International Narcotics and Law Enforcement (INL) Corrections System Support Program (CSSP) in Afghanistan** Objectives: Evaluate the effectiveness of CSSP in building a safe, secure, and humane prison system that meets international standards and Afghan cultural requirements, including whether INL is achieving intended and sustainable results through the following CSSP components: training and mentoring; capacity building; Counter-Narcotics Justice Center and Judicial Security Unit Compound operations and maintenance; Pol-i-Charkhi management and stabilization team; Central Prison Directorate engagement and reintegration team; and Kandahar expansion and support team. (Project: 12-AUD-030)	Dec-11	Sep-13	2 3 4
COPSWA Ref. No. 888 **Department of State Transition Planning for Reduced Military Presence in Afghanistan** Objective: Evaluate the Department of State transition planning for a reduced military presence in Afghanistan. (Project: 12-AUD-079)	Dec-12	Sep-13	11
COPSWA Ref. No. 972 **Audit of INL's Counternarcotics Programs in Afghanistan** Objective: Determine whether the Bureau of International Narcotics and Law Enforcement Affairs is achieving intended and sustainable results through its Counternarcotics Programs in Afghanistan. (Project: 13-AUD-082)	Jun-13	Dec-13	4
COPSWA Ref. No. 973 **Audit of Embassy Construction in Kabul** Objective: Determine whether the Department of State is effectively administering the Embassy construction contracts in Kabul. (Project: TBD)	Oct-13	Mar-14	9 10
COPSWA Ref. No. 974 **Audit of Bureau of Diplomatic Security Worldwide Protective Services (WPS) Contract Task Orders 2, 9, and 11 for Movement and Static Security Services in Jerusalem and Afghanistan** Objective: Determine whether the Department of State's administration and oversight of the WPS task order for KESF has been effective. (Project: 13-AUD-052)	Feb-13	Sep-13	10

Project	Start	Final	Strategic Issue
COPSWA Ref. No. 975 **Audit of the Closeout Process for Contracts Supporting the** **U.S. Mission in Afghanistan** Objective: Determine whether the Department of State was following prescribed procedures when closing out local and regional contracts in Afghanistan. (Project: TBD)	Nov-13	Jul-14	7 10
COPSWA Ref. No. 1178 **Audit of the Implementation of the Department of State Plan for** **the Transition From a Military-Led to a Civilian-Led Mission in** **Afghanistan** Objective: Determine whether the Department is effectively implementing its Afghanistan Transition Plan. (Project: TBD)	Nov-13	Jul-14	11
COPSWA Ref. No. 1179 **Audit of Property Accountability at U.S. Mission Afghanistan** Objective: Determine whether U.S. Mission Afghanistan has adequate controls in place over Embassy property to ensure that property is accurately recorded, monitored, and dispositioned. (Project: TBD)	May-14	Nov-14	9
COPSWA Ref. No. 1180 **Audit of the Aviation Working Capital Fund-Afghanistan** **Cost Center** Objective: Determine whether the Aviation Working Capital Fund for Afghanistan is effectively administered to ensure that costs and fees are distributed in an equitable manner. (Project: TBD)	May-14	Nov-14	10

U.S. Agency for International Development Office of Inspector General

Project	Start	Final	Strategic Issue
COPSWA Ref. No. 568 **ACA Financial Audit on Aircraft Charter Solutions** Objective: Under Embassy Air, 306-C-00-10-00510, for the period 02/01/2010 - 01/31/2011. (Project: FF200313)	Aug-12	Sep-13	10
COPSWA Ref. No. 577 **ACA Financial Audit on Development Alternatives, Inc.** Objective: Under Local Governance and Community Development Project (LGCD) - DFD-I-00-05-00250-00. (Project: FF200213)	Jan-13	Sep-13	2
COPSWA Ref. No. 579 **ACA Financial Audit on Tetra Tech Inc.** Objective: Under Kabul Electricity Service Improvement Program - EPP-I-06-03-00008-00. (Project: FF201013)	Apr-13	Oct-13	7
COPSWA Ref. No. 592 **ACA Financial Audit on Independent Directorate for** **Local Governance** Objective: Under District Delivery Program - 306-IL-10-04-01, for the period 01/14/2010 - 03/20/2012. (Project: FF200712)	May-12	Sep-13	2
COPSWA Ref. No. 599 **Review of USAID/Afghanistan's Management Controls Over Premium Pay** Objective: Determine if USAID/Afghanistan is using sufficient management controls over the submission, authorization, approval, and certification of premium pay benefits for its staff in accordance with Federal time and attendance policies and procedures. (Project: FF100612)	Sep-12	Oct-13	10
COPSWA Ref. No. 600 **Audit of USAID/Afghanistan's Transition Plans** Objective: Determine if USAID/Afghanistan developed measurable performance targets to be achieved by USAID programs by 2014 and assessed the capability of the Government of Afghanistan to sustain program accomplishments after 2014. (Project: FF100712)	Nov-12	Oct-13	11
COPSWA Ref. No. 604 **Audit of USAID/Afghanistan's Kandahar Power Initiative** Objective: Did USAID/Afghanistan adequately manage performance, plan for sustainability, and comply with environmental requirements in its management of the Kandahar Helmand Power Project? (Project: FF101112)	May-12	Sep-13	3

Project	Start	Final	Strategic Issue
COPSWA Ref. No. 738 **Review of USAID/Afghanistan's Use of the Commander's Emergency Response Program Funds for Selected Task Orders** Objective: Were the Commander's Emergency Response Program funds distributed by USFOR-A to USAID for specific projects used for their intended purposes and in compliance with applicable laws and regulations? (Project: FF101712)	Oct-11	Oct-13	3
COPSWA Ref. No. 743 **DCAA Financial Audit of the Louis Berger Group Inc. U.S. Costs - Year 1** Objective: Under Afghanistan Infrastructure Rehabilitation Program (AIRP), 306-I-00-06-00517-00, for the period 08/25/2006 - 09/30/2008. (Project: FF300311)	Jul-10	Oct-13	7
COPSWA Ref. No. 838 **ACA Financial Audit on International Foundation for Election Systems** Objective: Under Support to the Electoral Process (STEP), 306-DFD-I-06-05-00225-00, for the period 06/15/2008 - 11/21/2011. (Project: FF200713)	Jan-13	Oct-13	2
COPSWA Ref. No. 839 **ACA Financial Audit on Tetra Tech EM, Inc., Afghan Engineering Support Program (AESP)** Objective: Under 306-EDH-I-00-08-0002-00, for the period 11/09/2009 - 09/30/2011. (Project: FF201713)	Jul-13	Oct-13	7
COPSWA Ref. No. 843 **ACA Financial Audit on Development Alternatives, Inc.** Objective: Under Incentives Driving Economic Alternatives for the North, East, and West (IDEA-NEW), 306-A-00-09-00508-00, for the period 01/01/2010 - 12/31/2011. (Project: FF200913)	Mar-13	Oct-13	4
COPSWA Ref. No. 977 **Audit of USAID/Afghanistan's Afghanistan Election Assistance Program** Objectives: (1) Has USAID's assistance strengthened the ability of the Government of the Islamic Republic of Afghanistan institutions, Afghan civil society, and other organizations to enable credible, inclusive, and transparent presidential and provincial council elections in 2014? (2) Has USAID's assistance contributed to Afghan solutions to address the longer-term issues identified in the OIG's previous elections assistance audit (F-306-11-003-P)? (Project: FF100113)	Mar-13	Oct-13	2

Project	Start	Final	Strategic Issue
COPSWA Ref. No. 982 **Audit of USAID/Afghanistan's Financial Access for Investing in the Development of Afghanistan Project** Objective: Is the Financial Access for Investing in the Development of Afghanistan project effective in building a sustainable, diverse, and inclusive financial sector that can generate and sustain quality employment to meet the needs of micro, small, and medium enterprises throughout the country? (Project: FF100513)	Sep-13	Feb-14	2
COPSWA Ref. No. 987 **Audit of Gender-Related Activities in Selected USAID/Afghanistan Programs** Objectives: (1) How have gender issues been considered in designing, implementing, and measuring the performance of selected USAID/Afghanistan programs? (2) What impacts have these programs had on the health and educational status, economic development, and political empowerment of Afghan women and girls? (Project: FF101013)	Mar-14	Sep-14	2
COPSWA Ref. No. 1047 **ACA Financial Audit on Management Systems International** Objective: Under Afghanistan Anti-Corruption Authority (4A), 306-DFD-I-06-08-00072), for the period 10/01/2010 - 06/30/2012. (Project: FF200413)	Oct-12	Sep-13	5
COPSWA Ref. No. 1048 **ACA Financial Audit on Motion Matters Corporation** Objective: Under Afghanistan Media Development and Empowerment Project (AMDEP), 306-C-00-11-00517-00, for the period 02/23/2011 - 10/31/2011. (Project: FF200613)	Dec-12	Oct-13	3
COPSWA Ref. No. 1197 **ACA Financial Audit on Education Development Center** Objective: Under Skills Training for Afghan Youth (STAY), 306-A-00-10-00524-00, for the period 04/1/2010 - 12/31/2011. (Project: FF200813)	Jan-13	Sep-13	3
COPSWA Ref. No. 1198 **ACA Financial Audit on Ministry of Finance** Objective: Under Salary Support to GIRoA, 306-IL-10-06-0.1. (Project: FF201913)	Jan-13	Dec-13	2
COPSWA Ref. No. 1199 **ACA Financial Audit on Oasis International School, Inc.** Objective: Under Afghan Tuition Scholarship Program/ISK, 306-A-00-11-00528-00, for the period 08/21/2011 - 08/20/2013. (Project: FF201113)	Jun-13	Oct-13	2

Project	Start	Final	Strategic Issue
COPSWA Ref. No. 1200 **ACA Financial Audit on Consortium for Election and Political Process Strengthening** Objective: Under Support Increased Electoral Participation in Afghanistan, 306-A-00-08-00529-00, for the period 09/28/2008 - 09/30/2012. (Project: FF201213)	Jun-13	Oct-13	2
COPSWA Ref. No. 1201 **ACA Financial Audit on the ASIA Foundation** Objective: Under Strengthening Education in Afghanistan (SEA), 306-A-00-10-00530-00 /AID-306-A-00-10-00530, for the period 08/8/2010 - 09/30/2012. (Project: FF201313)	Jun-13	Oct-13	2
COPSWA Ref. No. 1202 **ACA Financial Audit on Ministry of Education** Objective: Under Basic Education, Literacy, and Technical-Vocational Education, 306-IL-12-07, for the period 11/16/2011 - 12/20/2012. (Project: FF201413)	Jun-13	Oct-13	2
COPSWA Ref. No. 1203 **ACA Financial Audit on Ministry of Agriculture, Irrigation, and Livestock** Objective: Under Agriculture Development Fund, 306-IL-12-OAG-16, for the period 07/18/2010 - 12/30/2013. (Project: FF201513)	Jun-13	Dec-13	2
COPSWA Ref. No. 1204 **ACA Financial Audit on Associates in Rural Development** Objective: Under Kabul City Initiative, 306-EPP-I-05-04-00035, for the period 10/1/2010 - 09/30/2013. (Project: FF201613)	Jun-13	Dec-13	2
COPSWA Ref. No. 1205 **ACA Financial Audit on Wildlife Conservation Society** Objective: Under Improving Livelihoods and Governance Through Natural Resource Management in Afghanistan (ILGNRM), 306-A-00-10-00516-00, for the period 04/10/2010 - 06/30/2013. (Project: FF201813)	Jul-13	Dec-13	2
COPSWA Ref. No. 1206 **ACA Financial Audit on Black & Veatch Special Projects Corporation** Objective: Under Kandahar-Helmand Power Program, 306-C-00-11-00506-00. (Project: TBD)	Jan-14	Apr-14	7
COPSWA Ref. No. 1207 **ACA Financial Audit on Education Development Center** Objective: Under Literacy & Community Empowerment Program, 306-A-00-04-00555-00. (Project: TBD)	Jan-14	Apr-14	2

Project	Start	Final	Strategic Issue
COPSWA Ref. No. 1208 **ACA Financial Audit on Citizen Network for Foreign Affairs** Objective: Under Afghanistan Farm Service Alliance (AFSA), 306-A-00-08-00517-00. (Project: TBD)	Jan-14	Apr-14	2
COPSWA Ref. No. 1209 **ACA Financial Audit on the Louis Berger Group Inc./Black & Veatch Joint Venture** Objective: Under Gardez to Khost Road, 306-I-08-06-00517-00. (Project: TBD)	Jan-14	Apr-14	7
COPSWA Ref. No. 1210 **ACA Financial Audit on Checchi & Company** Objective: Under Rule of Law Stabilization-Informal (RLS-I) – Bridge/Follow On Project, 306-DFD-I-05-04-00170. (Project: TBD)	Jan-14	Apr-14	2
COPSWA Ref. No. 1211 **ACA Financial Audit on Counterpart International, Inc.** Objective: Under Initiative to Promote Afghan Civil Society (IPACS II), 306-A-00-10-00534-00. (Project: TBD)	Jan-14	Apr-14	2
COPSWA Ref. No. 1212 **ACA Financial Audit on Development Alternatives, Inc.** Objective: Under Regional Afghan Municipalities Program for Urban Population (RAMP UP - RC EAST), 306-C-00-10-00526-00. (Project: TBD)	Jan-14	Apr-14	2
COPSWA Ref. No. 1213 **ACA Financial Audit on Development Alternatives, Inc.** Objective: Under Regional Afghan Municipalities Program for Urban Population (RAMP UP - RC West), 306-C-00-11-00501-00. (Project: TBD)	Jan-14	Apr-14	2
COPSWA Ref. No. 1214 **ACA Financial Audit on Development Alternatives, Inc.** Objective: Under Regional Afghan Municipalities Program for Urban Population (RAMP UP - RC North), 306-C-00-11-00510-00. (Project: TBD)	Jan-14	Apr-14	2
COPSWA Ref. No. 1215 **ACA Financial Audit on Deloitte Consulting, LLP** Objective: Under Afghan Civil Service Support Program (ACSS), 306-C-00-07-00508-00. (Project: TBD)	Jan-14	Apr-14	2
COPSWA Ref. No. 1216 **ACA Financial Audit on International Organization for Migration** Objective: Under Construction of Health and Education Facilities (CHEF), 306-A-00-08-00512-00. (Project: TBD)	Jan-14	Apr-14	2

Project	Start	Final	Strategic Issue
COPSWA Ref. No. 1217 **ACA Financial Audit on Purdue University** Objective: Under Strengthening Afghanistan Agricultural Faculties (SAAF), 306-A-00-11-00516-00. (Project: TBD)	Jan-14	Apr-14	2
COPSWA Ref. No. 1218 **ACA Financial Audit on the ASIA Foundation** Objective: Under Performance Based Governors' Fund (PBGF), 306-A-00-09-00531-00. (Project: TBD)	Jan-14	Apr-14	2
COPSWA Ref. No. 1219 **ACA Financial Audit on American University of** **Afghanistan (AUAF)** Objective: Under Support for the American University of Afghanistan, 306-A-00-08-00525-00. (Project: TBD)	Jan-14	Apr-14	2
COPSWA Ref. No. 1220 **ACA Financial Audit on the Research Foundation of State** **University of New York** Objective: Under Afghanistan Parliamentary Assistance Program (APAP I), 306-A-00-11-00518-00. (Project: TBD)	Jan-14	Apr-14	2
COPSWA Ref. No. 1221 **ACA Financial Audit on the Research Foundation of State** **University of New York** Objective: Under Afghanistan Parliamentary Assistance Program (APAP II), AID-306-C-12-00001. (Project: TBD)	Jan-14	Apr-14	2
COPSWA Ref. No. 1222 **ACA Financial Audit on Democracy International, Inc.** Objective: Under Electoral Reform and Civic Advocacy (AERCA), 306-A-00-09-00522-00. (Project: TBD)	Jan-14	Apr-14	2
COPSWA Ref. No. 1223 **ACA Financial Audit on University of Massachusetts** Objective: Under Higher Education Project in Afghanistan (HEP), 306-A-00-11-00515-00/AID-306-A-00-11-00515. (Project: TBD)	Jan-14	Apr-14	2
COPSWA Ref. No. 1224 **ACA Financial Audit on International Relief and Development** Objective: Under Engineering, Quality Assurance and Logistical Support (EQUALS), 306-C-00-11-00512-00. (Project: TBD)	Jan-14	Apr-14	7

Project	Start	Final	Strategic Issue
COPSWA Ref. No. 1225 **ACA Financial Audit on the ASIA Foundation** Objective: Under The Ministry of Women's Affairs Initiative to Strengthen Policy and Advocacy (MISPA)/Ministry of Woman Affairs (MOWA) - Strengthening policy and advocacy through communication and institution building, 306-A-00-06-00503-00. (Project: TBD)	Jan-14	Apr-14	2
COPSWA Ref. No. 1226 **ACA Financial Audit on AED-Academy for Educational Development** Objective: Under Higher Education Project in Afghanistan (HEP), 306-A-00-06-00506-00. (Project: TBD)	Jan-14	Apr-14	2
COPSWA Ref. No. 1227 **ACA Financial Audit on Tetra Tech EM, Inc.** Objective: Under Salang Tunnel Feasibility Study, AID-306-TO-12-00008. (Project: TBD)	Jan-14	Apr-14	7
COPSWA Ref. No. 1228 **ACA Financial Audit on Development Alternatives, Inc.** Objective: Under Agricultural Credit Enhancement (ACE) Program, 306-EDH-I-14-05-00004. (Project: TBD)	Jan-14	Apr-14	2
COPSWA Ref. No. 1229 **ACA Financial Audit on Consortium For Elections & Political Process Strengthening** Objective: Under Afghanistan Provincial Council Assistance (APCAP) vice - Support to Sub-National Governance Structures (SNG), 306-A-00-08-00513/AID-306-A-00-08-00513. (Project: TBD)	Jan-14	Apr-14	2
COPSWA Ref. No. 1230 **ACA Financial Audit on Checchi & Company** Objective: Under Rule of Law Stabilization - Informal Component, AID-306-C-12-00013. (Project: TBD)	Jan-14	Apr-14	2
COPSWA Ref. No. 1231 **ACA Financial Audit on Tetra Tech DPK** Objective: Under Rule of Law Stabilization - Formal Component, AID-306-C-12-00014. (Project: TBD)	Jan-14	Apr-14	2
COPSWA Ref. No. 1232 **ACA Financial Audit on Tetra Tech ARD** Objective: Under Land Reform in Afghanistan (LARA), 306-C-00-11-00514-00. (Project: TBD)	Jan-14	Apr-14	2

Project	Start	Final	Strategic Issue
COPSWA Ref. No. 1233 **ACA Financial Audit on Chemonics International, Inc.** Objective: Under Financial Access for Investing in the Development of Afghanistan - FAIDA, AID/306-C-00-11-00531-00. (Project: TBD)	Jan-14	Apr-14	2
COPSWA Ref. No. 1234 **ACA Financial Audit on Management Sciences for Health, Inc.** Objective: Under Strengthening Pharmaceutical Systems, 306-A-00-11-00532-00. (Project: TBD)	Jan-14	Apr-14	2
COPSWA Ref. No. 1235 **ACA Financial Audit on AECOM International Development, Inc.** Objective: Under Stabilization in Key Areas (SiKA) East Program, AID-306-C-12-00002. (Project: TBD)	Jan-14	Apr-14	2
COPSWA Ref. No. 1236 **ACA Financial Audit on AECOM International Development, Inc.** Objective: Under Stabilization in Key Areas (SiKA) West Program, AID-306-C-12-00004. (Project: TBD)	Jan-14	Apr-14	2
COPSWA Ref. No. 1237 **ACA Financial Audit on Development Alternatives, Inc.** Objective: Under Stabilization in Key Areas (SiKA) North, AID-306-C-12-00003. (Project: TBD)	Jan-14	Apr-14	2
COPSWA Ref. No. 1238 **ACA Financial Audit on Management Systems Information** Objective: Under Measuring Impact of Stabilization Initiative (MISTI), AID-306-TO-12-00004. (Project: TBD)	Jan-14	Apr-14	2
COPSWA Ref. No. 1239 **ACA Financial Audit on AECOM International Development, Inc.** Objective: Under Stabilization in Key Areas (SiKA) South Program, AID-306-C-12-00005. (Project: TBD)	Jan-14	Apr-14	2
COPSWA Ref. No. 1240 **ACA Financial Audit on International Relief and Development** Objective: Under Afghan Civilian Assistance Program (ACAP II), 306-A-00-11-00533-00. (Project: TBD)	Jan-14	Apr-14	2
COPSWA Ref. No. 1241 **ACA Financial Audit on ACS-Aircraft Charter Solutions, Inc.** **(Initially Norse Air)** Objective: Under USAID Air Support, 306-C-00-04-00558-00. (Project: TBD)	Jan-14	Apr-14	2

Project	Start	Final	Strategic Issue
COPSWA Ref. No. 1242 **ACA Financial Audit on MWH Americas, Inc.** Objective: Under Engineering Design Support Activity, 306-EDH-I-01-08-00025-00. (Project: TBD)	Jan-14	Apr-14	7
COPSWA Ref. No. 1243 **ACA Financial Audit on International City/County Mgmt. Assoc.** Objective: Under Commercialization of Afghanistan Water & Sanitation Activity (CAWSA), 306-A-00-09-00501-00. (Project: TBD)	Jan-14	Apr-14	2
COPSWA Ref. No. 1244 **ACA Financial Audit on Management Sciences for Health** Objective: Under Rural Expansion of Afghanistan's Community-Based Healthcare, EEE-C-00-03-00021-00. (Project: TBD)	Jan-14	Apr-14	2
COPSWA Ref. No. 1245 **ACA Financial Audit on Creative Associates International, Inc.** Objective: Under Afghanistan Primary Education Program, EEE-C-00-03-00008-00. (Project: TBD)	Jan-14	Apr-14	2
COPSWA Ref. No. 1246 **ACA Financial Audit on Center for Development and Population Activities** Objective: Under a Better Educated and Healthier Population, 306-GPH-C-00-01-00006. (Project: TBD)	Jan-14	Apr-14	2
COPSWA Ref. No. 1247 **ACA Financial Audit on Christian Children's Fund** Objective: Under Child Protection and Psychological Support for Afghan Children and Youth Program, EEE-A-00-03-00019-00. (Project: TBD)	Jan-14	Apr-14	2
COPSWA Ref. No. 1248 **ACA Financial Audit on Loma Linda University** Objective: Under Loma Linda University Support to Wazir Akbar Khan Hospital and Kabul Medical University, 306-A-00-07-00505-00. (Project: TBD)	Feb-14	May-14	2
COPSWA Ref. No. 1249 **ACA Financial Audit on Arzu, Inc.** Objective: Under Social Benefits Program for Afghan Women Weavers Future, 306-G-00-08-00524-00. (Project: TBD)	Feb-14	May-14	2
COPSWA Ref. No. 1250 **ACA Financial Audit on Chemonics International, Inc.** Objective: Under Rebuilding Agricultural Markets Program (RAMP) in Afghanistan, 306-C-00-03-00502-00. (Project: TBD)	Feb-14	May-14	2

Project	Start	Final	Strategic Issue
COPSWA Ref. No. 1251 **ACA Financial Audit on Cornell International Institute for Food, Agriculture, and Development** Objective: Under Private and Community Forestry for Natural Resource Management Sustainable Strategies for Village and Farmer Based Forestry Initiatives, 306-A-00-06-00531-00. (Project: TBD)	Feb-14	May-14	2
COPSWA Ref. No. 1252 **ACA Financial Audit on Association for Rural Development, Inc.** Objective: Under Afghanistan Local Governance Assistance Project (ALGAP), AEP-I-809-00-00016-00. (Project: TBD)	Feb-14	May-14	3
COPSWA Ref. No. 1253 **ACA Financial Audit on Consortium for Elections and Political Process Strengthening** Objective: Under Democracy and Governance in Afghanistan, DFD-A-00-03-00033-00. (Project: TBD)	Feb-14	May-14	2
COPSWA Ref. No. 1254 **ACA Financial Audit on Checchi & Company** Objective: Under Rule of Law Stabilization - Informal (RLS-I) – Bridge/Follow On Project, (PROAG 3060002.21). (Project: TBD)	Feb-14	May-14	2
COPSWA Ref. No. 1255 **ACA Financial Audit on Management Systems Information** Objective: Under Afghanistan Foreign Affairs Institutional Reform (FAIR) Project, 306-DFD-I-05-05-00221-00. (Project: TBD)	Feb-14	May-14	2
COPSWA Ref. No. 1256 **ACA Financial Audit on Tetra Tech ARD** Objective: Under Local Governance and Community Development (LGCD) Program - North and West, 306-DFD-I-00-05-00248-00. (Project: TBD)	Feb-14	May-14	2
COPSWA Ref. No. 1257 **ACA Financial Audit on AF Ferguson and Company** Objective: Under Third party monitoring for the Community Development Program, 306-C-00-09-00520-00. (Project: TBD)	Feb-14	May-14	2
COPSWA Ref. No. 1258 **ACA Financial Audit on Advance Engineering Associates, International** Objective: Under Training, Technical Assistance, and Capacity Enhancement to the Ministry of Mines (MoM), AID-306-TO-12-00002. (Project: TBD)	Feb-14	May-14	2

Project	Start	Final	Strategic Issue
COPSWA Ref. No. 1259 **ACA Financial Audit on Purdue University** Objective: Under Advancing Afghan Agriculture Alliance, 306-A-00-07-00509-00. (Project: TBD)	Feb-14	May-14	2
COPSWA Ref. No. 1260 **ACA Financial Audit on Chemonics International, Inc.** Objective: Under a Food Security Conditions and Causes study for Afghanistan, AID-AFP-I-02-05-00027. (Project: TBD)	Feb-14	May-14	2
COPSWA Ref. No. 1261 **ACA Financial Audit on Basic Support for Child Survival** Objective: Under Maternal and Child Health/Management Sciences for Health (MSH), 306-GHA-I-10-04-00002. (Project: TBD)	Feb-14	May-14	2
COPSWA Ref. No. 1262 **ACA Financial Audit on Air Serv International** Objective: Under Aviation Support Services, 306-G-00-03-00508-00. (Project: TBD)	Feb-14	May-14	2
COPSWA Ref. No. 1263 **ACA Financial Audit on CARE USA-Cooperative for Assistance and Relief Everywhere, Inc.** Objective: Under Urban Shelter in Afghanistan, DFD-A-00-06-00147-00. (Project: TBD)	Feb-14	May-14	2
COPSWA Ref. No. 1264 **ACA Financial Audit on International Resources Group** Objective: Under Cooperation for Peace and Security in Afghanistan and the Tribal Frontier (Peace and Security) program, AID-OAA-TO-11-00037. (Project: TBD)	Feb-14	May-14	2
COPSWA Ref. No. 1265 **RCA Financial Audit on Turquoise Mountain Trust** Objective: Under Urban Regeneration, Community Development, Education, and Business Development, 306-A-00-09-00503-00. (Project: TBD)	Feb-14	May-14	2
COPSWA Ref. No. 1266 **ACA Financial Audit on the GIRoA** Objective: Under Democratic Government With Broad Citizen Participation (Cash Transfer Assistance Agreement for Civil Service Reform), 306-06-00-01. (Project: TBD)	Feb-14	May-14	2
COPSWA Ref. No. 1267 **ACA Financial Audit on Deloitte Consulting, LLP** Objective: Under Economic Growth and Governance Initiative - EGGI, EEM-I-04-07-00005-00. (Project: TBD)	Feb-14	May-14	2

Project	Start	Final	Strategic Issue
COPSWA Ref. No. 1268 **ACA Financial Audit on GIRoA, Directorate of Local Governance (IDLG)** Objective: Under District Delivery Program (DDP), 306-IL-10-04-01. (Project: TBD)	Feb-14	May-14	2
COPSWA Ref. No. 1309 **Audit of USAID/Afghanistan's Afghanistan Civilian Assistance Program II (ACAP II)** Objective: Is USAID/Afghanistan's assistance through the Afghan Civilian Assistance Program II reaching its intended beneficiaries and having its intended impact? (Project: TBD)	Sep-13	Mar-14	2
COPSWA Ref. No. 1310 **Review of USAID/Afghanistan's Basic Education, Literacy, and Technical-Vocational Education (BELT)** Objective: Is USAID/Afghanistan's Basic Education, Literacy, and Technical-Vocational Education and Training program improving access to quality basic education, literacy, technical-vocational education and training for girls and other marginalized populations? (Project: TBD)	Oct-13	Apr-14	2
COPSWA Ref. No. 1311 **Audit of USAID's Afghanistan's Agriculture Development Fund (ADF)** Objective: Has USAID/Afghanistan's Agriculture Development Fund been managed to ensure that intended results are achieved? (Project: TBD)	Mar-14	Sep-14	2
COPSWA Ref. No. 1312 **Review of Government to Government Assistance** Objective: Are the financial controls associated with USAID/Afghanistan's government to government adequate and reliable? (Project: TBD)	Apr-14	Oct-14	6

U.S. Government Accountability Office

Project	Start	Final	Strategic Issue
COPSWA Ref. No. 1054 **Afghanistan Equipment Retrograde** Objectives: (1) To what extent has DoD implemented base closure procedures, including the accountability of equipment, to meet command established objectives and timelines? (2) To what extent are command established objectives and timelines for the Afghanistan equipment drawdown supported by DoD facilities and processes? (3) To what extent is DoD using cost and other information to help ensure it is making cost-effective disposition decisions? (Project: 351798)	Jan-13	Nov-13	9
COPSWA Ref. No. 1055 **Updated Review of U.S. Efforts to Address Attacks by Afghan Security Force Personnel on Members of the U.S. Military** Objectives: Examine the extent to which: (1) DoD and others have identified the causes of attacks by ANSF and impersonators on DoD personnel; (2) additional safeguards against attacks, if any that DoD and others have established since GAO's April 2012 review and the extent to which these safeguards have been implemented; and (3) what progress, if any, DoD has made in obtaining renewed access to the Afghan government's biometric and background information on ANSF candidates and personnel. (Project: 320962)	Jan-13	Sep-13	1
COPSWA Ref. No. 1132 **DoD Container Management** Objectives: To what extent (1) has DoD established and implemented corrective action plans to address its container management issues. (2) Do DoD container management processes provide for efficient and cost effective logistics operations in Afghanistan? (Project: 351805)	Mar-13	Mar-14	9
COPSWA Ref. No. 1135 **Costs of DoD's Transition to the Afghan Public Protection Force (APP)** Objectives: Examine the extent to which: (1) DoD implemented the transition of security services from private security contractors to the APPF; (2) DoD developed cost estimates related to the transition to the APPF and what actions are being taken to minimize these costs; and (3) DoD assessed the current and potential security risks to U.S. personnel and logistics as a result of the transition to the APPF and taken measures to minimize these risks. (Project: 351819)	May-13	TBD	10

Project	Start	Final	Strategic Issue
COPSWA Ref. No. 1166 **Department of State and U.S. Agency for International Development Contingency Contracting** Objectives: To what extent have State and USAID: (1) assessed their organizational structures related to contracting for overseas contingency operations and determined whether related changes are needed; (2) assessed their contract planning, management, and coordination policies for overseas contingency operations and determined whether changes to those policies are needed; and (3) assessed their acquisition workforce, including reliance on contractors, for overseas contingency operations and determined whether changes are needed? (Project: 121119)	Mar-13	Jan-14	10
COPSWA Ref. No. 1167 **The Department of Defense and State and USAID Use of Urgent and Compelling Exceptions to Competition** Objectives: (1) What is the pattern of DoD, State and Agency for International Development's use of this exception, including the range of goods and services acquired? (2) What processes do agencies have for reviewing justifications to use this exception? (3) For selected contracts awarded under this exception, to what extent (a) do the justifications meet Federal Acquisition Regulation requirements, (b) did agencies seek bids from more than one contractor and (c) did the contracts comply with requirements regarding the duration of contracts? (Project: 121124)	Mar-13	Jan-14	10
COPSWA Ref. No. 1168 **Security of Newly Acquired Diplomatic Facilities Overseas** Objectives: (1) How does State assess risk and establish physical security standards for acquired and temporary overseas facilities; (2) to what extent does State meet its security standards for such facilities; and (3) to what extent do State's policies and procedures mitigate vulnerabilities if such facilities do not meet security standards? (Project: 320966)	Mar-13	Feb-14	8
COPSWA Ref. No. 1169 **Department of Homeland Security (DHS) Efforts to Combat Terrorism Overseas** Objectives: (1) What DHS programs and resources contribute to U.S. efforts to combat terrorism?; (2) to what extent do DHS programs and resources abroad align with DHS and U.S. goals and priorities?; and (3) to what extent do U.S. embassies have mechanisms in place to use DHS knowledge and skills? (Project: 441113)	Oct-12	Sep-13	8

Project	Start	Final	Strategic Issue
COPSWA Ref. No. 1294 **Drawdown of DoD Contractors in Afghanistan** Objectives: Address (1) the extent to which DoD is applying operational contract support lessons learned as it begins its drawdown of contractors and their equipment in Afghanistan; (2) the processes established by DoD and USFOR-A to drawdown its contractor workforce and associated equipment and whether this process is consistent with established guidance; (3) the extent to which DoD is using cost and other information to help ensure it is making cost-effective operational contract support decisions, including decisions on the disposition of contractor-managed government-owned equipment; (4) actions the Department has taken to ensure that there are sufficient oversight personnel in place to oversee contractors as it reduces the number of military forces in Afghanistan; and (5) the extent to which DoD and USFOR-A have begun planning for the use of contractors after December 2014. In addition, GAO will identify the factors that are being considered as DoD begins to plan its post-2014 contractor requirements and what actions DoD is taking to ensure that the operational contractor support needed to support the post-2014 footprint is being provided in the most cost-effective manner possible. (Project: 351851)	Jul-13	Jan-14	10
COPSWA Ref. No. 1315 **Impact of U.S. Force Reductions on the Advising Mission in Afghanistan** Objectives: GAO will review DoD's efforts to support the advising mission in Afghanistan through December 2014, including: (1) To what extent has DoD identified the composition and missions of U.S. forces as it makes force reductions over the next year; (2) To what extent has DoD identified the support and security requirements for the remaining forces that will be engaged in the advising mission as force reductions occur; and (3) What challenges, if any, does DoD face in providing support and security for the advising mission, and what steps it has taken to mitigate any challenges? (Project: 351854)	Aug-13	TBD	11
COPSWA Ref. No. 1325 **Use of Foreign Labor Contractors Abroad** Objectives: (1) What are the practices of U.S. Government contractors in recruiting foreign workers for work outside the United States? (2) What legal and other authorities do U.S. agencies identify as providing protection to foreign workers employed by U.S. Government contractors outside the United States? (3) To what extent do Federal agencies provide oversight and enforcement of such authorities? (Project: 320985)	Jun-13	TBD	10

Project	Start	Final	Strategic Issue
COPSWA Ref. No. 1326 **Construction Efforts at the U.S. Embassy in Kabul** Objectives: (1) What progress has State made in constructing new U.S. embassy facilities in Kabul since 2009, and what factors have contributed to any scope, cost, or schedule changes? (2) To what extent have construction planning and implementation been conducted in conformance with State policies? (3) How did State determine its projected staffing levels and to what extent will planned construction meet or exceed these estimated needs? (Project: 320990)	Aug-13	TBD	11

Section 1.3. Afghanistan Projects by Strategic Oversight Issue

Strategic Oversight Issue No. 1: Building the Capacity and Capabilities of the Afghan National Security Forces and Administering and Maintaining Accountability of the Afghanistan Security Forces Fund

Project	COPSWA Page Number
Department of Defense Office of Inspector General	
COPSWA Ref. No. 668 **Shindand Training Contracts** (Project: D2013-D000AS-0052.000)	26
COPSWA Ref. No. 905 **Audit of the Surveillance Structure on Contracts Supporting the Afghanistan Rotary Wing Program for the U.S. Transportation Command** (Project: D2013-D000AS-0001.000) Note: Also appears in strategic oversight issue 10.	26
COPSWA Ref. No. 908 **Assessment of the U.S. Military and Coalition Efforts to Develop Effective and Sustainable Healthcare Capability for the ANP** (Project: D2013-D00SPO-0154.000)	27
COPSWA Ref. No. 911 **Assessment of Planning for the Effective Development/Transition of Critical ANSF Enablers to Post-2014 Capabilities** (Project: D2013-D00SPO-0087.000) Note: Also appears in strategic oversight issue 11.	27
COPSWA Ref. No. 912 **ANP Metrics Product** (Project: D2011-D00SPO-0182.007)	27
COPSWA Ref. No. 918 **ANA Metrics Product** (Project: D2011-D00SPO-0182.008)	28
COPSWA Ref. No. 1042 **Price Reasonableness Determinations for Datron World Communications, Inc. Contracts Awarded by the U.S. Army Contracting Command for the ANSF** (Project: D2013-D000AT-0083.000) Note: Also appears in strategic oversight issue 10.	29
COPSWA Ref. No. 1170 **Ministry of Defense/General Staff/ANA Logistics Development** (Project: SPO/TBD)	29
COPSWA Ref. No. 1171 **ANP Metrics Product** (Project: D2011-D00SPO-0182-009)	29

Project	COPSWA Page Number
COPSWA Ref. No. 1172 **ANA Metrics Product** (Project: D2011-D00SPO-0181.010)	29
COPSWA Ref. No. 1173 **Post-2014 ANSF Train and Equip** (Project: SPO/TBD)	30
Special Inspector General for Afghanistan Reconstruction	
COPSWA Ref. No. 823 **Base Construction Requirements and Transition Procedures for ANSF** (Project: SIGAR-069A)	37
COPSWA Ref. No. 950 **ANP Logistics Capability for Petroleum, Oil, and Lubricants (POL)** (Project: SIGAR-070A) Note: Also appears in strategic oversight issue 5.	37
COPSWA Ref. No. 959 **Contracts for ANSF Literacy Training** (Project: SIGAR-072A) Note: Also appears in strategic oversight issue 7.	38
COPSWA Ref. No. 1033 **DoD's Procurement and Management of Class IX (Automotive) Repair Parts for the ANSF** (Project: SIGAR-071A)	39
COPSWA Ref. No. 1059 **Reliability of ANSF Personnel Data** (Project: SIGAR-079A) Note: Also appears in strategic oversight issue 7.	39
COPSWA Ref. No. 1138 **Accountability of Weapons and Equipment Provided to the ANSF** (Project: SIGAR-A-078A) Note: Also appears in strategic oversight issue 7.	49
COPSWA Ref. No. 1177 **Mobile Strike Force Vehicles for the ANA** (Project: SIGAR-085A)	50
COPSWA Ref. No. 1295 **Review of Equipment Provided to the Afghan Air Force Through the FY 2014 ASFF** (Project: TBD)	51
COPSWA Ref. No. 1298 **Review of Cash and Local Payments for ANSF Fuel** (Project: TBD)	52
U.S. Government Accountability Office	
COPSWA Ref. No. 1055 **Updated Review of U.S. Efforts to Address Attacks by Afghan Security Force Personnel on Members of the U.S. Military** (Project: 320962)	70

Strategic Oversight Issue No. 2: Building Afghan Governance Capacity

Project	COPSWA Page Number
Special Inspector General for Afghanistan Reconstruction	
COPSWA Ref. No. 966 **U.S. Training of Afghan Justice Sector Personnel** (Project: SIGAR-073A) Note: Also appears in strategic oversight issue 7.	38
COPSWA Ref. No. 1075 **U.S. Government Reconstruction Transition Plan** (Project: SIGAR-080A) Note: Also appears in strategic oversight issue 11.	42
COPSWA Ref. No. 1130 **Assessments of Afghan Ministerial Capacity** (Project: SIGAR-A-081A) Note: Also appears in strategic oversight issue 6.	49
COPSWA Ref. No. 1137 **U.S. Efforts to Develop and Strengthen the Capacity of Afghanistan's Central Bank (DABS)** (Project: SIGAR-082A) Note: Also appears in strategic oversight issue 6.	49
COPSWA Ref. No. 1160 **Efforts to Increase Afghanistan's Capacity to Assess and Collect Customs Revenue** (Project: SIGAR-083A)	50
COPSWA Ref. No. 1283 **DoD's Use of Wire Transfers** (Project: SIGAR-084A)	51
COPSWA Ref. No. 1293 **Review of Education Projects in Afghanistan** (Project: SIGAR-086A)	51
COPSWA Ref. No. 1299 **USAID Afghanistan Municipal Programs** (Project: TBD)	52
COPSWA Ref. No. 1302 **Afghanistan Telecommunications** (Project: TBD)	53
COPSWA Ref. No. 1303 **National Solidarity Program III (NSP)** (Project: TBD)	53
Department of State Office of Inspector General	
COPSWA Ref. No. 545 **Audit of Bureau of International Narcotics and Law Enforcement (INL) Corrections System Support Program (CSSP) in Afghanistan** (Project: 12-AUD-030) Note: Also appears in strategic oversight issue 3 and 4.	56

Project	COPSWA Page Number
U.S. Agency for International Development Office of Inspector General	
COPSWA Ref. No. 577 **ACA Financial Audit on Development Alternatives, Inc.** (Project: FF200213)	58
COPSWA Ref. No. 592 **ACA Financial Audit on Independent Directorate for Local Governance** (Project: FF200712)	58
COPSWA Ref. No. 838 **IFES-International Foundation for Election Systems** (Project: FF200713)	59
COPSWA Ref. No. 977 **Audit of USAID/Afghanistan's Afghanistan Election Assistance Program** (Project: FF100113)	59
COPSWA Ref. No. 982 **Audit of USAID/Afghanistan's Financial Assistance for Investing in the Development of Afghanistan Project** (Project: FF100513)	60
COPSWA Ref. No. 987 **Audit of Gender-Related Activities in Selected USAID/Afghanistan Programs** (Project: FF101013)	60
COPSWA Ref. No. 1198 **ACA Financial Audit on Ministry of Finance** (Project: TBD)	60
COPSWA Ref. No. 1199 **ACA Financial Audit on Oasis International School, Inc.** (Project: FF201113)	60
COPSWA Ref. No. 1200 **ACA Financial Audit on Consortium For Election and Political Process Strengthening** (Project: FF201213)	61
COPSWA Ref. No. 1201 **ACA Financial Audit on the ASIA Foundation** (Project: FF201313)	61
COPSWA Ref. No. 1202 **ACA Financial Audit on Ministry of Education** (Project: FF201413)	61
COPSWA Ref. No. 1203 **ACA Financial Audit on Ministry of Agriculture, Irrigation, and Livestock** (Project: FF201513)	61
COPSWA Ref. No. 1204 **ACA Financial Audit on Associates in Rural Development** (Project: FF201613)	61
COPSWA Ref. No. 1205 **ACA Financial Audit on Wildlife Conservation Society** (Project: FF201813)	61

Project	COPSWA Page Number
COPSWA Ref. No. 1207 **ACA Financial Audit on Education Development Centre (EDC)** (Project: TBD)	61
COPSWA Ref. No. 1208 **ACA Financial Audit on Citizen Network for Foreign Affairs** (Project: TBD)	62
COPSWA Ref. No. 1210 **ACA Financial Audit on Checchi & Company** (Project: TBD)	62
COPSWA Ref. No. 1211 **ACA Financial Audit on Counterpart International, Inc. (CI)** (Project: TBD)	62
COPSWA Ref. No. 1212 **ACA Financial Audit on Development Alternatives, Inc.** (Project: TBD)	62
COPSWA Ref. No. 1213 **ACA Financial Audit on Development Alternatives, Inc.** (Project: TBD)	62
COPSWA Ref. No. 1214 **ACA Financial Audit on Development Alternatives, Inc.** (Project: TBD)	62
COPSWA Ref. No. 1215 **ACA Financial Audit on Deloitte Consulting, LLP** (Project: TBD)	62
COPSWA Ref. No. 1216 **ACA Financial Audit on International Organization for Migration** (Project: TBD)	62
COPSWA Ref. No. 1217 **ACA Financial Audit on Purdue University** (Project: TBD)	63
COPSWA Ref. No. 1218 **ACA Financial Audit on the ASIA Foundation** (Project: TBD)	63
COPSWA Ref. No. 1219 **ACA Financial Audit on American University of Afghanistan (AUAF)** (Project: TBD)	63
COPSWA Ref. No. 1220 **ACA Financial Audit on the Research Foundation of State University of New York** (Project: TBD)	63
COPSWA Ref. No. 1221 **ACA Financial Audit on the Research Foundation of State University of New York** (Project: TBD)	63
COPSWA Ref. No. 1222 **ACA Financial Audit on Democracy International, Inc.** Project: TBD	63

Project	COPSWA Page Number
COPSWA Ref. No. 1223 **ACA Financial Audit on University of Massachusetts** (Project: TBD	63
COPSWA Ref. No. 1225 **ACA Financial Audit on the ASIA Foundation** (Project: TBD)	64
COPSWA Ref. No. 1226 **ACA Financial Audit on AED-Academy for Educational Development** (Project: TBD)	64
COPSWA Ref. No. 1228 **ACA Financial Audit on Development Alternatives, Inc.** (Project: TBD)	64
COPSWA Ref. No. 1229 **ACA Financial Audit on Consortium for Elections & Political Process Strengthening** (Project: TBD)	64
COPSWA Ref. No. 1230 **ACA Financial Audit on Checchi & Company** (Project: TBD)	64
COPSWA Ref. No. 1231 **ACA Financial Audit on Tetra Tech DPK** (Project: TBD)	64
COPSWA Ref. No. 1232 **ACA Financial Audit on Tetra Tech ARD** (Project: TBD)	64
COPSWA Ref. No. 1233 **ACA Financial Audit on Chemonics International, Inc.** (Project: TBD)	65
COPSWA Ref. No. 1234 **ACA Financial Audit on Management Sciences for Health, Inc.** (Project: TBD)	65
COPSWA Ref. No. 1235 **ACA Financial Audit on AECOM International Development, Inc.** (Project: TBD)	65
COPSWA Ref. No. 1236 **ACA Financial Audit on AECOM International Development, Inc.** (Project: TBD)	65
COPSWA Ref. No. 1237 **ACA Financial Audit on Development Alternatives, Inc.** (Project: TBD)	65
COPSWA Ref. No. 1238 **ACA Financial Audit on Management Systems Information** (Project: TBD)	65
COPSWA Ref. No. 1239 **ACA Financial Audit on AECOM International Development, Inc.** (Project: TBD)	65

Project	COPSWA Page Number
COPSWA Ref. No. 1240 **ACA Financial Audit on International Relief and Development** (Project: TBD)	65
COPSWA Ref. No. 1241 **ACA Financial Audit on ACS-Aircraft Charter Solutions, Inc. (Initially Norse Air)** (Project: TBD)	65
COPSWA Ref. No. 1243 **ACA Financial Audit on International City/County Mgmt. Assoc.** (Project: TBD)	66
COPSWA Ref. No. 1244 **ACA Financial Audit on Management Sciences for Health** (Project: TBD)	66
COPSWA Ref. No. 1245 **ACA Financial Audit on Creative Associates International, Inc.** (Project: TBD)	66
COPSWA Ref. No. 1246 **ACA Financial Audit on Center for Development and Population Activities** (Project: TBD)	66
COPSWA Ref. No. 1247 **ACA Financial Audit on Christian Children's Fund** (Project: TBD)	66
COPSWA Ref. No. 1248 **ACA Financial Audit on Loma Linda University** (Project: TBD)	66
COPSWA Ref. No. 1249 **ACA Financial Audit on Arzu, Inc.** (Project: TBD)	66
COPSWA Ref. No. 1250 **ACA Financial Audit on Chemonics International, Inc.** (Project: TBD)	66
COPSWA Ref. No. 1251 **ACA Financial Audit on Cornell International Institute for Food, Agriculture, and Development** (Project: TBD)	67
COPSWA Ref. No. 1253 **ACA Financial Audit on Consortium For Elections and Political Process Strengthening** (Project: TBD)	67
COPSWA Ref. No. 1254 **ACA Financial Audit on Checchi & Company** (Project: TBD)	67
COPSWA Ref. No. 1255 **ACA Financial Audit on Management Systems Information** (Project: TBD)	67

Project	COPSWA Page Number
COPSWA Ref. No. 1256 **ACA Financial Audit on Tetra Tech ARD** (Project: TBD)	67
COPSWA Ref. No. 1257 **ACA Financial Audit on AF Ferguson and Company** (Project: TBD)	67
COPSWA Ref. No. 1258 **ACA Financial Audit on Advance Engineering Associates, International** (Project: TBD)	67
COPSWA Ref. No. 1259 **ACA Financial Audit on Purdue University** (Project: TBD)	68
COPSWA Ref. No. 1260 **ACA Financial Audit on Chemonics International, Inc.** (Project: TBD)	68
COPSWA Ref. No. 1261 **ACA Financial Audit on Basic Support for Child Survival** (Project: TBD)	68
COPSWA Ref. No. 1262 **ACA Financial Audit on Air Serv International** (Project: TBD)	68
COPSWA Ref. No. 1263 **ACA Financial Audit on CARE USA-Cooperative for Assistance and Relief Everywhere, Inc.** (Project: TBD)	68
COPSWA Ref. No. 1264 **ACA Financial Audit on International Resources Group** (Project: TBD)	68
COPSWA Ref. No. 1265 **RCA Financial Audit on Turquoise Mountain Trust** (Project: TBD)	68
COPSWA Ref. No. 1266 **ACA Financial Audit on the GIRoA** (Project: TBD)	68
COPSWA Ref. No. 1267 **ACA Financial Audit on Deloitte Consulting LLP** (Project: TBD)	68
COPSWA Ref. No. 1268 **ACA Financial Audit on the GIRoA, Directorate of Local Governance (IDLG)** (Project: TBD)	69
COPSWA Ref. No. 1309 **Audit of USAID/Afghanistan's Afghanistan Civilian Assistance Program II (ACAP II)** (Project: TBD)	69

Project	COPSWA Page Number
COPSWA Ref. No. 1310 **Review of USAID/Afghanistan's Basic Education, Literacy, and Technical-Vocational Education (BELT)** (Project: TBD)	69
COPSWA Ref. No. 1311 **Audit of USAID's Afghanistan's Agriculture Development Fund (ADF)** (Project: TBD)	69

Strategic Oversight Issue No. 3: Sustaining U.S. Investment in Afghan Institutions and Infrastructure

Project	COPSWA Page Number
Special Inspector General for Afghanistan Reconstruction	
COPSWA Ref. No. 1074 **USAID Assistance to Afghanistan's Water Sector** (Project: SIGAR-077A)	41
COPSWA Ref. No. 1085 **Inspections of Medical, Education, and Police Facilities in Kabul Province** **(Gardez Hospital)** (Project: SIGAR-I-005A) Note: Also appears in strategic oversight issue 7.	42
COPSWA Ref. No. 1087 **Inspections of Medical, Education, and Police Facilities in Kabul Province** **(Veayer Ahmad School)** (Project: SIGAR-I-005C) Note: Also appears in strategic oversight issue 7.	43
COPSWA Ref. No. 1090 **Inspections of Medical, Education, and Police Facilities in Kabul Province** **(Walayatti Clinic)** (Project: SIGAR-I-005F) Note: Also appears in strategic oversight issue 7.	43
COPSWA Ref. No. 1091 **Inspections of Medical, Education, and Police Facilities in Kabul Province** **(Paghman Clinic)** (Project: SIGAR-I-005H) Note: Also appears in strategic oversight issue 7.	43
COPSWA Ref. No. 1092 **Inspections of Medical, Education, and Police Facilities in Kabul Province** **(AOB SOF Clinic)** (Project: SIGAR-I-005I) Note: Also appears in strategic oversight issue 7.	43
COPSWA Ref. No. 1093 **Inspection of the Deh-e Sabz Slaughterhouse in Kabul Province** (Project: SIGAR-I-005J) Note: Also appears in strategic oversight issue 7.	43
COPSWA Ref. No. 1094 **Inspections of Medical, Education, and Police Facilities in Kabul Province** **(Ministry of Defense Headquarters)** (Project: SIGAR-I-005K) Note: Also appears in strategic oversight issue 7.	44

Project	COPSWA Page Number
COPSWA Ref. No. 1095 **Inspections of Medical, Education, and Police Facilities in the Northern Provinces (Archi District Police HQ)** (Project: SIGAR-I-006B) Note: Also appears in strategic oversight issue 7.	44
COPSWA Ref. No. 1103 **Inspections of Medical, Education, and Police Facilities in the Northern Provinces (3rd Kandak Monitor)** (Project: SIGAR-I-006L) Note: Also appears in strategic oversight issue 7.	44
COPSWA Ref. No. 1107 **Inspections of Medical, Education, and Police Facilities in the Northern Provinces (TTF MeS)** (Project: SIGAR-I-006P) Note: Also appears in strategic oversight issue 7.	44
COPSWA Ref. No. 1109 **Inspections of Medical, Education, and Police Facilities in the Northern Provinces (UP Prov. HQ Pole Khumri)** (Project: SIGAR-I-006R) Note: Also appears in strategic oversight issue 7.	45
COPSWA Ref. No. 1110 **Inspections of Medical, Education, and Police Facilities in the Northern Provinces (UP Dist. HQ Pole Khumri)** (Project: SIGAR-I-006S) Note: Also appears in strategic oversight issue 7.	45
COPSWA Ref. No. 1111 **Inspections of Medical, Education, and Police Facilities in the Northern Provinces (Provincial Response Co.)** (Project: SIGAR-I-006T) Note: Also appears in strategic oversight issue 7.	45
COPSWA Ref. No. 1112 **Inspections of Medical, Education, and Police Facilities in the Northern Provinces (ANCOP Patrol BN)** (Project: SIGAR-I-006U) Note: Also appears in strategic oversight issue 7.	45
COPSWA Ref. No. 1116 **Inspections of Incinerators (Ghazni)** (Project: SIGAR I-007B)	46
COPSWA Ref. No. 1117 **Inspections of Incinerators (Shank)** (Project: SIGAR I-007C)	46
COPSWA Ref. No. 1118 **Inspections of Incinerators (Sharana)** (Project: SIGAR I-007D)	46
COPSWA Ref. No. 1119 **Inspections of Incinerators (Bagram)** (Project: SIGAR I-007E)	46

Project	COPSWA Page Number
COPSWA Ref. No. 1120 **Inspections of Incinerators (Kandahar)** (Project: SIGAR I-007F)	46
COPSWA Ref. No. 1122 **Inspections of Medical, Education, Police, and Agricultural Facilities in the Western Provinces** (Project: SIGAR-I-008A) Note: Also appears in strategic oversight issue 7.	47
COPSWA Ref. No. 1123 **Inspections of Medical, Education, Police, and Agricultural Facilities in the Western Provinces** (Project: SIGAR-I-008B) Note: Also appears in strategic oversight issue 7.	47
COPSWA Ref. No. 1124 **Inspections of Medical, Education, Police, and Agricultural Facilities in the Western Provinces** (Project: SIGAR-I-008C) Note: Also appears in strategic oversight issue 7.	47
COPSWA Ref. No. 1125 **Inspections of Medical, Education, Police, and Agricultural Facilities in the Western Provinces** (Project: SIGAR-I-008D) Note: Also appears in strategic oversight issue 7.	47
COPSWA Ref. No. 1126 **Inspection of the Kajaki Dam and Related Construction Projects in Helmand Province (1 of 4 inspections)** (Project. SIGAR-I-009A) Note: Also appears in strategic oversight issue 7.	48
COPSWA Ref. No. 1127 **Inspection of the Kajaki Dam and Related Construction Projects in Helmand Province (2 of 4 inspections)** (Project: SIGAR-I-009B) Note: Also appears in strategic oversight issue 7.	48
COPSWA Ref. No. 1128 **Inspection of the Kajaki Dam and Related Construction Projects in Helmand Province (3 of 4 inspections)** (Project: SIGAR-I-009C) Note: Also appears in strategic oversight issue 7.	48
COPSWA Ref. No. 1129 **Inspection of the Kajaki Dam and Related Construction Projects in Helmand Province (4 of 4 inspections)** (Project: SIGAR-I-009D) Note: Also appears in strategic oversight issue 7.	48

Project	COPSWA Page Number
COPSWA Ref. No. 1158 **Inspection of the Justice Center in Parwan (JCIP) Court House Construction Project in Regional Command East, Afghanistan** (Project: SIGAR-I-010) Note: Also appears in strategic oversight issue 7.	50
COPSWA Ref. No. 1290 **Audit of Afghan Women's Initiatives Funded by the U.S. Government** (Project: 087A)	51
COPSWA Ref. No. 1316 **Inspections of Medical, Education, and Police Facilities in Kabul Province (Camp Commando)** (Project: SIGAR-I-005L) Note: Also appears in strategic oversight issue 7.	53
Department of State Office of Inspector General	
COPSWA Ref. No. 545 **Audit of Bureau of International Narcotics and Law Enforcement (INL) Corrections System Support Program (CSSP) in Afghanistan** (Project: 12-AUD-030) Note: Also appears in strategic oversight issue 2 and 4.	56
U.S. Agency for International Development Office of Inspector General	
COPSWA Ref. No. 604 **Audit of USAID/Afghanistan's Kandahar Power Initiative** (Project: FF101112)	58
COPSWA Ref. No. 738 **Review of USAID/Afghanistan's Use of the Commander's Emergency Response Program Funds for Selected Task Orders** (Project: FF101712)	59
COPSWA Ref. No. 1048 **ACA Financial Audit on Motion Matters Corporation** (Project: FF200613)	60
COPSWA Ref. No. 1197 **ACA Financial Audit on Education Development Center** (Project: FF200813)	60
COPSWA Ref. No. 1252 **ARD-Association For Rural Development, Inc.** (Project: TBD)	67

Strategic Oversight Issue No. 4: Executing and Sustaining
Counternarcotics Programs

Project	COPSWA Page Number
Special Inspector General for Afghanistan Reconstruction	
COPSWA Ref. No. 1297 **Effectiveness of U.S. Counternarcotics Programs** (Project: TBD)	52
Department of State Office of Inspector General	
COPSWA Ref. No. 545 **Audit of Bureau of International Narcotics and Law Enforcement (INL)** **Corrections System Support Program (CSSP) in Afghanistan** (Project: 12-AUD-030) Note: Also appears in strategic oversight issue 2 and 3.	56
COPSWA Ref. No. 972 **Audit of INL's Counternarcotics Programs in Afghanistan** (Project: 13-AUD-082)	56
U.S. Agency for International Development Office of Inspector General	
COPSWA Ref. No. 843 **ACA Financial Audit on Development Alternatives, Inc.** (Project: FF200913)	59

Strategic Oversight Issue No. 5: Implementing Anti-Corruption Initiatives

Project	COPSWA Page Number
Special Inspector General for Afghanistan Reconstruction	
COPSWA Ref. No. 950 **ANP Logistics Capability for Petroleum, Oil, and Lubricants (POL)** (Project: SIGAR-070A) Note: Also appears in strategic oversight issue 1.	37
COPSWA Ref. No. 967 **Rule of Law Programs-Outcomes and Sustainability** (Project: TBD)	38
COPSWA Ref. No. 1056 **Evaluation of Progress Made in Meeting U.S. Anti-Corruption Goals in Afghanistan** (Project: SIGAR-SP-6)	39
U.S. Agency for International Development Office of Inspector General	
COPSWA Ref. No. 1047 **ACA Financial Audit on Management Systems International** (Project: FF200413)	60

Strategic Oversight Issue No. 6: Planning, Coordinating, and Providing Stewardship of Direct and Indirect Assistance Funds and Programs

Project	COPSWA Page Number
Department of Defense Office of Inspector General	
COPSWA Ref. No. 914 **Examination of Department of Defense Execution of NATO Contributing Countries Donations to ANA Trust Fund for Approved Sustainment Projects, as of September 30, 2012** (Project: D2013-D000FL-0056.000)	28
Special Inspector General for Afghanistan Reconstruction	
COPSWA Ref. No. 1082 **Afghan Ministries of Defense and Interior Affairs Capacity Assessments** (Project: SIGAR SP-12)	42
COPSWA Ref. No. 1130 **Assessments of Afghan Ministerial Capacity** (Project: SIGAR-A-081A) Note: Also appears in strategic oversight issue 2.	49
COPSWA Ref. No. 1137 **U.S. Efforts to Develop and Strengthen the Capacity of Afghanistan's Central Bank (DABS)** (Project: SIGAR-082A) Note: Also appears in strategic oversight issue 2.	49
COPSWA Ref. No. 1157 **Direct Assistance to the Da Afghanistan Breshna Sherkat (DABS) for the Kajaki Dam Project** (Project: SIGAR-SP-10)	49
U.S. Agency for International Development Office of Inspector General	
COPSWA Ref. No. 1312 **Review of Government to Government Assistance** (Project: TBD)	69

Strategic Oversight Issue No. 7: Awarding and Administering Reconstruction Contracts

Project	COPSWA Page Number
Special Inspector General for Afghanistan Reconstruction	
COPSWA Ref. No. 937 **USAID's Direct Assistance to the Afghan Ministry of Public Health (MoPH) for Public Hospitals** (Project: SIGAR-068A)	37
COPSWA Ref. No. 959 **Contracts for ANSF Literacy Training** (Project: SIGAR-072A) Note: Also appears in strategic oversight issue 1.	38
COPSWA Ref. No. 966 **U.S. Training of Afghan Justice Sector Personnel** (Project: SIGAR-073A) Note: Also appears in strategic oversight issue 2.	38
COPSWA Ref. No. 1059 **Reliability of ANSF Personnel Data** (Project: SIGAR-079A) Note: Also appears in strategic oversight issue 1.	39
COPSWA Ref. No. 1061 **Financial Audit of USAID Cooperative Agreement 306-A-00-09-00511-00 With Central Asia Development Group (CADG) for the Community Development Program (CDP)** (Project: SIGAR F-013)	39
COPSWA Ref. No. 1062 **Financial Audit of USAID Contracts 306-M-00-07-00502-00 and 306-DFD-I-04-00170-00 With Checchi and Company Consulting, Inc. for Results Tracking Services and Rule of Law Stabilization Program** (Project: SIGAR F-014)	39
COPSWA Ref. No. 1063 **Financial Audit of USAID Contract 306-M-00-06-00508-00 and Cooperative Agreement 306-A-00-10-00513-00 With Creative Associates International for the Building Education Support System for Teachers (BESST) and the Community Based Stabilization (CBSG) Programs** (Project: SIGAR F-015)	40
COPSWA Ref. No. 1064 **Financial Audit of USAID Cooperative Agreement 306-A-00-06-00523-00 With JHPIEGO Corp. for the Health Service Support Project (HSSP)** (Project: SIGAR F-016)	40
COPSWA Ref. No. 1065 **Financial Audit of USAID Cooperative Agreement 306-A-00-09-00512-00 With Mercy Corps for the Community Development Program (CDP) in Balkh, Kunduz, Baghlan, and Bamyan** (Project: SIGAR F-017)	40

Project	COPSWA Page Number
COPSWA Ref. No. 1066 **Financial Audit of USAID Cooperative Agreement 306-A-00-09-00510-00 With CARE International for the Community Development Program (CDP) in Kabul** (Project: SIGAR F-018)	40
COPSWA Ref. No. 1067 **Financial Audit of USAID Contract 306-C-00-09-00531-00 With World Council of Credit Unions for the Rural Finance and Cooperative Development (RUFCOD) Program** (Project: SIGAR F-019)	40
COPSWA Ref. No. 1068 **Financial Audit of USAID Cooperative Agreement 306-A-00-05-00511-00 With Counterpart International, Inc. for the Initiative to Promote Afghan Civil Society (IPACS I) Program** (Project: SIGAR F-020)	40
COPSWA Ref. No. 1069 **Financial Audit of USAID Contract 306-EPP-I-11-03-00006-00 With International Resources Group for the Afghan Clean Energy Program (ACEP)** (Project: SIGAR F-032)	41
COPSWA Ref. No. 1070 **Financial Audit of USAID Cooperative Agreement 306-A-00-09-00513-00 With World Vision for the Community Development Program (CDP) in Herat, Qala-i-Naw, Chaghcharan** (Project: SIGAR F-021)	41
COPSWA Ref. No. 1071 **Financial Audit of Various Department of State Grants to Afghan Technical Consultants for the Removal of Land Mines and Unexploded Ordnance** (Project: SIGAR F-022)	41
COPSWA Ref. No. 1085 **Inspections of Medical, Education, and Police Facilities in Kabul Province (Gardez Hospital)** (Project: SIGAR-I-005A) Note: Also appears in strategic oversight issue 3.	42
COPSWA Ref. No. 1087 **Inspections of Medical, Education, and Police Facilities in Kabul Province (Veayer Ahmad School)** (Project: SIGAR-I-005C) Note: Also appears in strategic oversight issue 3.	43
COPSWA Ref. No. 1090 **Inspections of Medical, Education, and Police Facilities in Kabul Province (Walayatti Clinic)** (Project: SIGAR-I-005F) Note: Also appears in strategic oversight issue 3.	43
COPSWA Ref. No. 1091 **Inspections of Medical, Education, and Police Facilities in Kabul Province (Paghman Clinic)** (Project: SIGAR-I-005H) Note: Also appears in strategic oversight issue 3.	43

Project	COPSWA Page Number
COPSWA Ref. No. 1092 **Inspections of Medical, Education, and Police Facilities in Kabul Province (AOB SOF Clinic)** (Project: SIGAR-I-005I) Note: Also appears in strategic oversight issue 3.	43
COPSWA Ref. No. 1093 **Inspection of the Deh-e Sabz Slaughterhouse in Kabul Province** (Project: SIGAR-I-005J) Note: Also appears in strategic oversight issue 3.	43
COPSWA Ref. No. 1094 **Inspections of Medical, Education, and Police Facilities in Kabul Province (Ministry of Defense Headquarters)** (Project: SIGAR-I-005K) Note: Also appears in strategic oversight issue 3.	44
COPSWA Ref. No. 1095 **Inspections of Medical, Education, and Police Facilities in the Northern Provinces (Archi District Police HQ)** (Project: SIGAR-I-006B) Note: Also appears in strategic oversight issue 3.	44
COPSWA Ref. No. 1103 **Inspections of Medical, Education, and Police Facilities in the Northern Provinces (3rd Kandak Monitor)** (Project: SIGAR-I-006L) Note: Also appears in strategic oversight issue 3.	44
COPSWA Ref. No. 1107 **Inspections of Medical, Education, and Police Facilities in the Northern Provinces (TTF MeS)** (Project: SIGAR-I-006P) Note: Also appears in strategic oversight issue 3.	44
COPSWA Ref. No. 1109 **Inspections of Medical, Education, and Police Facilities in the Northern Provinces (UP Prov. HQ Pole Khumri)** (Project: SIGAR-I-006R) Note: Also appears in strategic oversight issue 3.	45
COPSWA Ref. No. 1110 **Inspections of Medical, Education, and Police Facilities in the Northern Provinces (UP Dist. HQ Pole Khumri)** (Project: SIGAR-I-006S) Note: Also appears in strategic oversight issue 3.	45
COPSWA Ref. No. 1111 **Inspections of Medical, Education, and Police Facilities in the Northern Provinces (Provincial Response Co.)** (Project: SIGAR-I-006T) Note: Also appears in strategic oversight issue 3.	45

Project	COPSWA Page Number
COPSWA Ref. No. 1112 **Inspections of Medical, Education, and Police Facilities in the Northern Provinces (ANCOP Patrol BN)** (Project: SIGAR-I-006U) Note: Also appears in strategic oversight issue 3.	45
COPSWA Ref. No. 1122 **Inspections of Medical, Education, Police, and Agricultural Facilities in the Western Provinces** (Project: SIGAR-I-008A) Note: Also appears in strategic oversight issue 3.	47
COPSWA Ref. No. 1123 **Inspections of Medical, Education, Police, and Agricultural Facilities in the Western Provinces** (Project: SIGAR-I-008B) Note: Also appears in strategic oversight issue 3.	47
COPSWA Ref. No. 1124 **Inspections of Medical, Education, Police, and Agricultural Facilities in the Western Provinces** (Project: SIGAR-I-008C) Note: Also appears in strategic oversight issue 3.	47
COPSWA Ref. No. 1125 **Inspections of Medical, Education, Police, and Agricultural Facilities in the Western Provinces** (Project: SIGAR-I-008D) Note: Also appears in strategic oversight issue 3.	47
COPSWA Ref. No. 1126 **Inspection of the Kajaki Dam and Related Construction Projects in Helmand Province (1 of 4 inspections)** (Project: SIGAR-I-009A) Note: Also appears in strategic oversight issue 3.	48
COPSWA Ref. No. 1127 **Inspection of the Kajaki Dam and Related Construction Projects in Helmand Province (2 of 4 inspections)** (Project: SIGAR-I-009B) Note: Also appears in strategic oversight issue 3.	48
COPSWA Ref. No. 1128 **Inspection of the Kajaki Dam and Related Construction Projects in Helmand Province (3 of 4 inspections)** (Project: SIGAR-I-009C) Note: Also appears in strategic oversight issue 3.	48
COPSWA Ref. No. 1129 **Inspection of the Kajaki Dam and Related Construction Projects in Helmand Province (4 of 4 inspections)** (Project: SIGAR-I-009D) Note: Also appears in strategic oversight issue 3.	48

Project	COPSWA Page Number
COPSWA Ref. No. 1136 **Financial Audit of Costs Incurred Under Cooperative Agreement** **306-A-00-08-00509-00 With International Relief and Development, Inc. the** **Strategic Provincial Roads – Southern and Eastern Afghanistan Project** (Project: SIGAR-F-012)	49
COPSWA Ref. No. 1138 **Accountability of Weapons and Equipment Provided to the ANSF** (Project: SIGAR-A-078A) Note: Also appears in strategic oversight issue 1.	49
COPSWA Ref. No. 1158 **Inspection of the Justice Center in Parwan (JCIP) Court House Construction** **Project in Regional Command East, Afghanistan** (Project: SIGAR-I-010) Note: Also appears in strategic oversight issue 3.	50
COPSWA Ref. No. 1164 **Financial Audit of USAID Contracts 306-C-00-07-00503-00** **and 306-DOT-I-02-08-00035-00 With Development Alternatives, Inc. for the** **Afghanistan Small and Medium Enterprise Development & Afghanistan** **Stabilization Initiative Programs** (Project: SIGAR-F-023)	50
COPSWA Ref. No. 1165 **Financial Audit of USAID Contracts 306-DOT-I-01-08-00033-00 and** **306-C-00-07-00501-00 With Chemonics International, Inc. for the Afghanistan** **Stabilization Initiative & Accelerated Sustainable Agriculture Programs** (Project: SIGAR-F-024)	50
COPSWA Ref. No. 1300 **USAID Afghan Info Database** (Project: TBD)	52
COPSWA Ref. No. 1301 **USAID's Measuring Impact of Stabilization Initiative (MISTI)** (Project: TBD)	52
COPSWA Ref. No. 1304 **Use of Third-Party Monitoring by USAID** (Project: TBD)	53
COPSWA Ref. No. 1316 **Inspections of Medical, Education, and Police Facilities in Kabul Province** **(Camp Commando)** (Project: SIGAR-I-005L). Note: Also appears in strategic oversight issue 3.	53
COPSWA Ref. No. 1327 **Financial Audit of USAID Contract 306-DFD-A-00-00304-00 With International** **Relief and Development for the Afghanistan Vouchers for Increased Production in** **Agriculture Program** (Project: SIGAR-F-025)	53

Project	COPSWA Page Number
COPSWA Ref. No. 1328 **Financial Audit of USAID Contract EPP-I-05-04-00019-00 With ARD, Inc. for the Sustainable Water Supply and Sanitation Project** (Project: SIGAR-F-026)	53
COPSWA Ref. No. 1329 **Financial Audit of USAID Contract 306-A-00-06-00519-00 With PACT for Media Development in Afghanistan** (Project: SIGAR-F-027)	54
COPSWA Ref. No. 1330 **Financial Audit of USAID Contract 306-DFD-I-03-05-00125-00 AECOM for the Afghanistan Social Outreach Program** (Project: SIGAR-F-028)	54
COPSWA Ref. No. 1331 **Financial Audit of USAID Contract 306-A-00-06-00518-00 With CARE USA for the Partnership for Advancing Community Based Education in Afghanistan** (Project: SIGAR-F-029)	54
COPSWA Ref. No. 1332 **Financial Audit of USAID Contract 306-DFD-I-09-04-00173-00 With Tetra Tech DPK for Rule of Law Stabilization Program Formal Local Governance Program** (Project: SIGAR-F-030)	54
COPSWA Ref. No. 1333 **Financial Audit of USAID Contract 306-A-00-07-00514-00 With International City Managers Association for the Afghanistan Municipal Strengthening Program** (Project: SIGAR-F-031)	54
COPSWA Ref. No. 1334 **Financial Audit USAID Contract 306-EPP-I-11-03-00006-00 With International Resources Group for the Afghan Clean Energy Program** (Project: SIGAR- F-032)	54
COPSWA Ref. No. 1335 **Financial Audit of DOS/INL Contract SAQMPD05F2737 With Pacific Architects & Engineers (PAE) for the Afghan Clean Energy Program** (Project: SIGAR-F-033)	54
COPSWA Ref. No. 1336 **Financial Audit of Various Department of State Instruments With the Mine Clearance Planning Agency for Humanitarian Mine and UXO Clearance** (Project: SIGAR-F-034)	55
COPSWA Ref. No. 1337 **Financial Audit of DOS PAS Contracts SAF20010CA014 and SAF20011GR142 With CETENA Group for Public Diplomacy** (Project: SIGAR-F-035)	55
COPSWA Ref. No. 1338 **Financial Audit of DOS PAS Contract SAF20011CA026 With Sayed Majidi Architecture and Design (SMAD) for Public Diplomacy** (Project: SIGAR-F-036)	55

Project	COPSWA Page Number
Department of State Office of Inspector General	
COPSWA Ref. No. 975 **Audit of the Closeout Process for Contracts Supporting the U.S. Mission in Afghanistan** (Project: TBD) Note: Also appears in strategic oversight issue 10.	57
U.S. Agency for International Development Office of Inspector General	
COPSWA Ref. No. 579 **ACA Financial Audit on Tetra Tech Inc.** (Project: FF201013)	58
COPSWA Ref. No. 743 **DCAA Financial Audit of the Louis Berger Group Inc. U.S. Costs - Year 1** (Project: FF300311)	59
COPSWA Ref. No. 839 **ACA Financial Audit on Tetra Tech EM, Inc., Afghan Engineering Support Program (AESP)** (Project: FF201713)	59
COPSWA Ref. No. 1206 **ACA Financial Audit on Black & Veatch Special Projects Corporation** (Project: TBD)	61
COPSWA Ref. No. 1209 **ACA Financial Audit on the Louis Berger Group Inc./Black & Veatch Joint Venture** (Project: TBD)	62
COPSWA Ref. No. 1224 **ACA Financial Audit on International Relief and Development** (Project: TBD)	63
COPSWA Ref. No. 1227 **ACA Financial Audit on Tetra Tech EM, Inc.** (Project: TBD)	64
COPSWA Ref. No. 1242 **ACA Financial Audit on MWH Americas, Inc.** (Project: TBD)	66

Strategic Oversight Issue No. 8: Health and Safety

Project	COPSWA Page Number
U.S. Army Audit Agency	
COPSWA Ref. No. 1034 **Force Protection-Base Access Controls** (Project: A-2013-MTE-0135.000)	32
U.S. Government Accountability Office	
COPSWA Ref. No. 1168 **Security of Newly Acquired Diplomatic Facilities Overseas** (Project: 320966)	71
COPSWA Ref. No. 1169 **Department of Homeland Security Efforts to Combat Terrorism Overseas** (Project: 441113)	71

In addition to the Afghanistan-specific oversight projects above, the following are CONUS-based projects included in Section 2 of the COPSWA that provide more broad-based oversight coverage related to health and safety.

Project	COPSWA Page Number
Department of Defense Office of Inspector General	
COPSWA Ref. No. 1020 **Assessment of DoD Wounded Warrior Matters - Addressing Risks Involved in Managing Multiple Medications** (Project: D2009-D00SPO-0209.005)	105
COPSWA Ref. No. 1021 **Assessment of DoD Wounded Warrior Matters - Selection and Training of Commanders and Cadre of Warrior Transition Units** (Project: D2009-D00SPO-0209.007)	106
COPSWA Ref. No. 1324 **Access to DoD Healthcare by Members of the U.S. Army Reserve Components** (Project: D2013-D00SPO-0212.000)	108
Naval Audit Service	
COPSWA Ref. No. 721 **USN Program 9 Synchronization With USMC Mobilization** (Project: 2012-076)	110

Strategic Oversight Issue No. 9: Retrograde and Property Management

Project	COPSWA Page Number
Department of Defense Office of Inspector General	
COPSWA Ref. No. 913 **Redistribution Property Assistance Team Operations in Afghanistan** (Project: D2013-D000JB-0133.000)	27
COPSWA Ref. No. 915 **Controls Over the Disposition of Equipment at the Defense Logistics Agency Disposition Services in Afghanistan** (Project: D2013-D000JB-0129.000)	28
COPSWA Ref. No. 1076 **Audit of the Security and Handling of Equipment Staged for Retrograde at Aerial Ports of Debarkation in Afghanistan** (Project: D2013-D000JB-0149.000)	29
COPSWA Ref. No. 1284 **Property Losses in Afghanistan** (Project: AUD/TBD)	30
COPSWA Ref. No. 1285 **Retrograde of Force Provider Equipment** (Project: AUD/TBD)	30
COPSWA Ref. No. 1291 **Afghanistan Base Closure and Facilities Management** (Project: AUD/TBD) Note: Also appears in strategic oversight issue 10.	30
U.S. Army Audit Agency	
COPSWA Ref. No. 923 **Retrograde of Class V in Afghanistan** (Project: A-2013-MTE-0139.000)	32
COPSWA Ref. No. 1036 **Management of Materiel Handling Equipment** (Project: A-2013-MTE-0137.000)	32
COPSWA Ref. No. 1078 **Repatriating Loaned Equipment** (Project: A-2013-MTE-0241.000)	33
COPSWA Ref. No. 1080 **Retrograde of Sensitive Equipment and Materiel** (Project: TBD)	33
U.S. Air Force Audit Agency	
COPSWA Ref. No. 896 **Remote Piloted Aircraft Maintenance and Accountability** (Project: F2012-O30000-0846)	35
COPSWA Ref. No. 931 **Afghanistan Base Closure Plans** (Project: F2013-O30000-0032)	35

Project	COPSWA Page Number
COPSWA Ref. No. 932 **Patient Movement Items (PMI)** (Project: F2013-O40000-0042)	35
COPSWA Ref. No. 1077 **Mission Capability (MICAP) Parts** (Project: F2013-L40000-0533.000)	35
COPSWA Ref. No. 1189 **Follow-Up Audit, Pallets** (Project: F2013-L40000-0962.000)	35
COPSWA Ref. No. 1190 **Air Force Equipment Management Systems (AFEMS) Accuracy** (Project: TBD)	36
COPSWA Ref. No. 1191 **Wireless Network Security** (Project: TBD)	36
COPSWA Ref. No. 1192 **Moral Network Operations** (Project: TBD)	36
COPSWA Ref. No. 1193 **Bulk Fuel Management** (Project: TBD)	36
COPSWA Ref. No. 1194 **Follow-Up, AFCENT War Reserved Materiel (WRM)** (Project: TBD)	36
COPSWA Ref. No. 1195 **Inter-theater Airlift Supporting CENTCOM** (Project: TBD)	36
Department of State Office of Inspector General	
COPSWA Ref. No. 973 **Audit of Embassy Construction in Kabul** (Project: TBD) Note: Also appears in strategic oversight issue 10.	56
COPSWA Ref. No. 1179 **Audit of Property Accountability at U.S. Mission Afghanistan** (Project: TBD)	57
U.S. Government Accountability Office	
COPSWA Ref. No. 1054 **Afghanistan Equipment Retrograde** (Project: 351798)	70
COPSWA Ref. No. 1132 **DoD Container Management** (Project: 351805)	70

Strategic Oversight Issue No. 10: Contract Management and Oversight

Project	COPSWA Page Number
Department of Defense Office of Inspector General	
COPSWA Ref. No. 905 **Audit of the Surveillance Structure on Contracts Supporting the Afghanistan Rotary Wing Program for the U.S. Transportation Command** (Project: D2013-D000AS-0001.000) Note: Also appears in strategic oversight issue 1.	26
COPSWA Ref. No. 906 **Information Operations Assessments in Afghanistan** (Project: D2012-D000JA-0223.000)	26
COPSWA Ref. No. 907 **Contract Oversight of Military Construction Projects for the Special Operations Forces Complexes at Bagram Airfield, Afghanistan** (Project: D2012-D000JO-0221.000)	26
COPSWA Ref. No. 1042 **Price Reasonableness Determinations for Datron World Communications, Inc. Contracts Awarded by the U.S. Army Contracting Command for the ANSF** (Project: D2013-D000AT-0083.000) Note: Also appears in strategic oversight issue 1.	29
COPSWA Ref. No. 1286 **ANSF Mi-17, Mi-35, AN-26, and AN-32 Aircraft Spare Parts - Accountability** (Project: AUD/TBD) Note: Also appears in strategic oversight issue 11.	30
COPSWA Ref. No. 1287 **Afghan Air Force Light Air Support Aircraft - Contract Administration** (Project: AUD/TBD) Note: Also appears in strategic oversight issue 11.	30
COPSWA Ref. No. 1291 **Afghanistan Base Closure and Facilities Management** (Project: AUD/TBD) Note: Also appears in strategic oversight issue 9.	30
COPSWA Ref. No. 1292 **Contracting Support in Afghanistan** (Project: AUD/TBD)	31
COPSWA Ref. No. 1321 **ANSF Mi-17, Mi-35, AN-26, and AN-32 Aircraft Spare Parts - Requirements** (Project: AUD/TBD) Note: Also appears in strategic oversight issue 11.	31
COPSWA Ref. No. 1322 **Afghan Air Force Light Air Support Aircraft - Contract Oversight** (Project: AUD/TBD) Note: Also appears in strategic oversight issue 11.	31

Project	COPSWA Page Number
U.S. Army Audit Agency	
COPSWA Ref. No. 882 **LOGCAP IV-Managing Drawdown** (Project: A-2012-MTE-0424.000)	32
COPSWA Ref. No. 1035 **Force Protection-Contractor Accountability** (Project: A-2013-MTE-0138.000)	32
COPSWA Ref. No. 1079 **Contract Drawdown** (Project: A-2013-MTE-0240.000)	33
COPSWA Ref. No. 1081 **Surface Tender CENTCOM Region (STCR) Program** (Project: A-2013-MTE-0239.000)	33
COPSWA Ref. No. 1131 **Linguist Contract Requirements** (Project: A-2013-FMI-0107.000)	33
Department of State Office of Inspector General	
COPSWA Ref. No. 973 **Audit of Embassy Construction in Kabul** (Project: TBD) Note: Also appears in strategic oversight issue 9	56
COPSWA Ref. No. 974 **Audit of Bureau of Diplomatic Security Worldwide Protective Services Contract Task Orders 2, 9, and 11 for Movement and Static Security Services in Jerusalem and Afghanistan** (Project: 13-AUD-052)	56
COPSWA Ref. No. 975 **Audit of the Closeout Process for Contracts Supporting the U.S. Mission in Afghanistan** (Project: TBD) Note: Also appears in strategic oversight issue 7.	57
COPSWA Ref. No. 1180 **Audit of the Aviation Working Capital Fund-Afghanistan Cost Center** (Project: TBD)	57
U.S. Agency for International Development Office of Inspector General	
COPSWA Ref. No. 568 **ACA Financial Audit on Aircraft Charter Solutions** (Project: FF200313)	58
COPSWA Ref. No. 599 **Review of USAID/Afghanistan's Management Controls Over Premium Pay** (Project: FF100612)	58

Project	COPSWA Page Number
U.S. Government Accountability Office	
COPSWA Ref. No. 1135 **Costs of DoD's Transition to the Afghan Public Protection Force** (Project: 351819)	70
COPSWA Ref. No. 1166 **Department of State and U.S. Agency for International Development Contingency Contracting** (Project: 121119)	71
COPSWA Ref. No. 1167 **The Department of Defense and State and USAID Use of Urgent and Compelling Exceptions to Competition** (Project: 121124)	71
COPSWA Ref. No. 1294 **Drawdown of DoD Contractors in Afghanistan** (Project No. 351851)	72
COPSWA Ref. No. 1325 **Use of Foreign Labor Contractors Abroad** (Project: 320985)	72

Strategic Oversight Issue No. 11: Transition Planning and Execution

Project	COPSWA Page Number
Department of Defense Office of Inspector General	
COPSWA Ref. No. 911 **Assessment of Planning for the Effective Development/Transition of Critical ANSF Enablers to Post-2014 Capabilities** (Project: D2013-D00SPO-0087.000) Note: Also appears in strategic oversight issue 1.	27
COPSWA Ref. No. 916 **Assessment of U.S. Government Efforts to Transition Security Cooperation and Assistance Activities Supporting the GIRoA From DoD Authority to DOS Authority** (Project: D2013-D00SPO-0181.000)	28
COPSWA Ref. No. 919 **Audit of the Transition of Facilities to the Logistics Civil Augmentation Program IV Density List at Kandahar Airfield, Afghanistan** (Project: D2013-D000JB-0050.000)	29
COPSWA Ref. No. 1286 **ANSF Mi-17, Mi-35, AN-26, and AN-32 Aircraft Spare Parts - Accountability** (Project: AUD/TBD) Note: Also appears in strategic oversight issue 10.	30
COPSWA Ref. No. 1287 **Afghan Air Force Light Air Support Aircraft - Contract Administration** (Project: AUD/TBD) Note: Also appears in strategic oversight issue 10.	30
COPSWA Ref. No. 1321 **ANSF Mi-17, Mi-35, AN-26, and AN-32 Aircraft Spare Parts - Requirements** (Project: AUD/TBD) Note: Also appears in strategic oversight issue 10.	31
COPSWA Ref. No. 1322 **Afghan Air Force Light Air Support Aircraft - Contract Oversight** (Project: AUD/TBD) Note: Also appears in strategic oversight issue 10.	31
Naval Audit Service	
COPSWA Ref. No. 168 **Marine Reserve Mobilization Orders** (Project: N2011-NMC000-0105.000)	34
COPSWA Ref. No. 184 **Navy Individual Augmentee Reintegration Process** (Project: 2012-070)	34

Project	COPSWA Page Number
Special Inspector General for Afghanistan Reconstruction	
COPSWA Ref. No. 1075 **U.S. Government Reconstruction Transition Plan** (Project: SIGAR-080A) Note: Also appears in strategic oversight issue 2.	42
Department of State Office of Inspector General	
COPSWA Ref. No. 888 **Department of State Transition Planning for Reduced Military Presence in Afghanistan** (Project: 12-AUD-079)	56
COPSWA Ref. No. 1178 **Audit of the Implementation of the Department of State Plan for the Transition From a Military-Led to a Civilian-Led Mission in Afghanistan** (Project: TBD)	57
U.S. Agency for International Development Office of Inspector General	
COPSWA Ref. No. 600 **Audit of USAID/Afghanistan's Transition Plans** (Project: FF100712)	58
U.S. Government Accountability Office	
COPSWA Ref. No. 1315 **Impact of U.S. Force Reductions on the Advising Mission in Afghanistan** (Project: 351854)	72
COPSWA Ref. No. 1326 **Construction Efforts at the U.S. Embassy in Kabul** (Project: 320990)	73

Section 2. Southwest Asia Projects Other Than Afghanistan

Department of Defense Office of Inspector General

Project	Start	Final	Country Code
COPSWA Ref. No. 850 **Controls Over Cash and Other Monetary Assets at Overseas Army Finance Command Disbursing Operations** Objective: Determine whether internal controls for Army General Fund, Cash and Other Monetary Assets held at selected Army disbursing sites located outside the continental United States (OCONUS) were effectively designed and operating adequately to safeguard, account, document, and report Cash and Other Monetary Assets. In addition, evaluate whether the Army Finance Command effectively implemented technical oversight and assisted Army disbursing sites that previously did not have oversight by an Army Financial Management Center. (Project: D2011-D000FP-0260.001)	Feb-12	Nov-13	KW SA
COPSWA Ref. No. 989 **DoD OIG Assessment of the Office of Security Cooperation-Iraq Mission Capability Project** Objective: Assess the adequacy of DoD support for executing security cooperation programs in Iraq and whether the Office of Security Cooperation-Iraq (OSC-I) is organized, equipped, and prepared to successfully accomplish its security cooperation mission. (Project: D2012-D00SPO-0205.000)	Aug-12	Sep-13	IQ
COPSWA Ref. No. 991 **Naval Support Activity Bahrain Military Construction Planning** Objective: Determine the requirements development and planning for military construction projects at Naval Support Activity Bahrain. Specifically, to determine whether the requirements development and planning processes resulted in requirements that meet DoD's needs. (Project: AUD/TBD)	Oct-13	Jul-14	BH
COPSWA Ref. No. 1020 **Assessment of DoD Wounded Warrior Matters - Addressing Risks Involved in Managing Multiple Medications** Objective: Determine whether the DoD programs for the care, management, and transition of recovering wounded Service members are managed effectively and efficiently. This is the fifth in a series of assessments on Wounded Warrior matters. (Project: D2009-D00SPO-0209.005)	Feb-12	Sep-13	CONUS

Project	Start	Final	Country Code
COPSWA Ref. No. 1021 **Assessment of DoD Wounded Warrior Matters - Selection and Training of Commanders and Cadre of Warrior Transition Units** Objective: Determine whether the DoD programs for the care, management, and transition of recovering wounded Service members are managed effectively and efficiently. This is the sixth in a series of assessments on Wounded Warrior matters. (Project: D2009-D00SPO-0209.007)	Apr-12	Oct-13	CONUS
COPSWA Ref. No. 1024 **Naval Support Activity Bahrain Military Construction Contract Administration** Objective: Determine whether the U.S. Army Corps of Engineers awarded Naval Support Activity Bahrain military construction projects in accordance with Federal and DoD regulations. Specifically, to determine whether officials are using appropriate contracting processes to satisfy Naval Support Activity Bahrain military construction project requirements. (Project: AUD/TBD)	Oct-13	Jul-14	BH
COPSWA Ref. No. 1049 **Mi-17 Cockpit Modifications Under Task Order W58RGZ-09-D-0130-0102** Objective: The DoD OIG continues its series of audits of the Mi-17 program. In this current audit, DoD OIG will determine whether DoD officials properly awarded and administered indefinite-delivery, indefinite-quantity contract W58RGZ-09-D-0130, task order 0102, for the modification of DoD-owned Mi-17 variant aircraft in accordance with Federal and DoD regulations and policies. Report No. DODIG-2013-123 addresses the procurement of overhaul services awarded by modification to Task Order 0102. (Project: D2013-D000AS-0097.000)	Feb-13	Oct-13	CONUS
COPSWA Ref. No. 1083 **Multimodal Locations in Southwest Asia** Objective: Determine whether effective procedures are in place to process equipment at transfer locations in Southwest Asia. (Project: D2013-D000JA-0155.000)	Apr-13	Mar-14	AE
COPSWA Ref. No. 1084 **Contract Administration for Installation Support Operations at Camp As Sayliyah** Objective: Determine whether DoD officials are properly administering the Camp As Sayliyah, Qatar, Base Operations Support Services Contract. Specifically, we will determine whether DoD officials are effectively reviewing contractor invoices and purchase requests before approval. This is the second in a series of reports on the Camp As Sayliyah, Qatar Base Operations Support Services Contract. Also see COPSWA Ref. No. 897. (Project: D2013-D000JB-0106.000)	Apr-13	Jan-14	QA

Project	Start	Final	Country Code
COPSWA Ref. No. 1174 **Assessment of DoD Suicide Event Report (DoDSER)** **Data Accuracy** Objective: Assess the extent that incomplete or inaccurate data from the DoD Suicide Event Report may have been used when making program or policy decisions on suicide prevention efforts and to determine the reason for the high number of "Don't Know" responses in some DoD Suicide Event Report data fields. (Project: D2013-D00SPO-0183.000)	Jun-13	Apr-14	CONUS
COPSWA Ref. No. 1175 **International Security Assistance - Training and Equipping** **Foreign Military Forces With "Section 1206" Funding** Objective: Determine if the "Section 1206" global train and equip program is achieving intended purposes, if it unnecessarily duplicates related U.S. Government counterterrorism programs, and if there are opportunities to save money. (Project: SPO/TBD)	Sep-13	Jul-14	BH EG KZ KG LB PK YE
COPSWA Ref. No. 1176 **Assessment of DoD Suicide Prevention Programs** Objective: Evaluate the Defense Suicide Prevention Program and assess DoD's oversight of Suicide Prevention policies and programs. The assessment will primarily address the implementation of key DoD Task Force recommendations. Specifically, the assessment will focus on whether there is a coordinated effort to plan, program, and execute a DoD suicide prevention program. (Project: SPO/TBD)	Oct-13	Jul-14	CONUS
COPSWA Ref. No. 1296 **Handling of Equipment at a Transfer Location in Southwest Asia** Objective: The DoD OIG is continuing its series of audits regarding U.S. Transportation Command's support of the Afghanistan drawdown. The first audit (Report No. DODIG-2013-066) addressed the U.S. Transportation Command's plan to support the drawdown of equipment from Afghanistan. The second audit (Project No. D2013-D000JA-0155.000) focuses on procedures used to process equipment at a commercial multimodal transfer location in Southwest Asia. In this third audit, DoD OIG will determine whether effective procedures are in place for processing equipment and materiel, including sensitive equipment, in Southwest Asia. (Project: D2013-D000RF-0209.000)	Aug-13	Mar-14	OTHER

Project	Start	Final	Country Code
COPSWA Ref. No. 1324 **Access to DoD Healthcare by Members of the U.S. Army Reserve Components** Objective: (1) Determine whether DoD-provided healthcare supports medical and dental readiness effectively and efficiently such that Reserve Component units and members are able to comply with required medical and dental standards pre-activation through deactivation to provide operational capabilities and strategic depth to meet U.S. defense requirements. (2) Determine whether DoD-provided healthcare provides effective and efficient care for wounded, ill, and injured National Guardsmen and Reservists' medical, dental, and mental health requirements. (Project: D2013-D00SPO-0212.000)	Oct-13	Aug-14	CONUS

U.S. Army Audit Agency

Project	Start	Final	Country Code
COPSWA Ref. No. 872 **Contractor Stock Fund Purchases Southwest Asia** Objectives: Verify that: (1) management controls over contractor stock fund purchases are in place and operating to ensure contractor purchases are in accordance with contract requirements, properly accounted for, and appropriately reimbursed, if required by contract and (2) supplies and materiel acquired outside the Army supply system with stock funds were authorized and properly accounted for. (Project: A-2012-MTE-0416.000)	Jun-12	Sep-13	KW QA
COPSWA Ref. No. 1038 **Contract Requirements for the Base Operations Support Contract-Kuwait** Objective: Verify contract requirements for the Base Operations Support and Security Contract in Kuwait were revalidated in accordance with the Federal Acquisition Regulation and appropriately adjusted to fit the current and projected base populations and footprint. (Project: A-2013-MTE-0136.000)	Jan-13	Oct-13	KW

Naval Audit Service

PROJECT	START	FINAL	Country Code
COPSWA Ref. No. 168 **Marine Reserve Mobilization Orders** Objective: Verify that internal controls provide reasonable assurance that Marine Corps Reserve CONUS mobilization orders are properly authorized, performed, and paid in accordance with applicable directives. (Project: N2011-NMC000-0105.000)	Jul-11	Sep-13	AF IQ
COPSWA Ref. No. 184 **Navy Individual Augmentee (IA) Reintegration Process** Objective: Verify that Navy Individual Augmentees are provided the intended support throughout the deployment cycle to reintegrate with family, community, and employers. (Project: 2012-070)	Dec-11	Oct-13	AF IQ
COPSWA Ref. No. 721 **USN Program 9 Synchronization With USMC Mobilization** Objective: Verify that current USN Program 9/Health and Safety Program (HASP) Corpsman support procedures and policies are synchronized with USMC mobilization timelines as intended. (Project: 2012-076)	Jun-12	Nov-13	CONUS
COPSWA Ref. No. 1025 **Fleet Gapped Critical Billets** Objective: Verify that internal controls over mission critical shipboard billets ensure manning requirements are met and billets are not gapped. (Project: 2012-049)	Aug-12	Oct-13	CONUS OCONUS

U.S. Air Force Audit Agency

PROJECT	START	FINAL	Country Code
COPSWA Ref. No. 896 **Remote Piloted Aircraft Maintenance and Accountability** Objective: Evaluate whether the Air Force effectively managed remote piloted aircraft. Specifically, assess whether personnel developed and maintained unit type codes addressing current mission needs, timely accomplished maintenance actions, and properly accounted for assets. (Project: F2012-O30000-0846)	Jul-12	Sep-13	AF KW AE
COPSWA Ref. No. 932 **Patient Movement Items (PMI)** Objectives: Determine whether Air Force Medical Service officials effectively manage patient movement items. Specifically, determine whether medical officials properly: (1) establish and fund equipment requirements and (2) maintain and account for patient movement items. (Project: F2013-O40000-0042)	Oct-13	Sep-14	AF KG QA
COPSWA Ref. No. 1077 **Mission Capability (MICAP) Parts** Objectives: Determine if Air Force Logistics personnel effectively managed mission capability parts. Specifically, determine if logistics personnel (1) properly supported and accurately documented mission capability parts requisitions and (2) properly processed and timely satisfied mission capability parts requirements. (Project: F2013-L40000-0533.000)	Mar-13	Sep-14	AF QA KG SA
COPSWA Ref. No. 1189 **Follow-Up Audit, Pallets** Objective: Determine if management implemented corrective actions in response to AFAA Audit Report F2009-0006-FC4000, February 4, 2009. Specifically, determine if management implemented actions to accurately compute pallet requirements, maintain accurate pallet inventory data, and implement an effective retrograde program. (Project: F2013-L40000-0962.000)	Jul-13	Jul-14	AF QA JO OM AE BH
COPSWA Ref. No. 1190 **Air Force Equipment Management Systems (AFEMS) Accuracy** Objective: Determine if personnel effectively managed AFEMS data. Specifically, determine if logistics personnel accurately recorded item data, accurately accounted for equipment items in AFEMS, and consistently reported information between AFEMS and the Standard Base Supply System. (Project: TBD)	May-14	May-15	AF QA KG

PROJECT	START	FINAL	Country Code
COPSWA Ref. No. 1191 **Wireless Network Security** **Objective:** Evaluate management of Second Generation Wireless Local Area network (2GWLAN) security in the AFCENT AOR. Specifically, determine whether Air Force officials effectively manage wireless network and device authorization, configuration, and operation. (Project: TBD)	May-14	May-15	AF QA KG
COPSWA Ref. No. 1192 **Moral Network Operations** **Objective:** Determine whether Air Force Central Command personnel effectively and efficiently manage the Moral Network in deployed locations. Specifically, determine if management properly locates moral networks in authorized common areas, properly funds moral networks, and effectively performs contract administration when required. (Project: TBD)	May-14	May-15	AF QA KG
COPSWA Ref. No. 1193 **Bulk Fuel Management** **Objective:** Evaluate bulk fuel management in the AFCENT Southwest Asia AOR. Specifically, determine whether the Air Force accurately accounts for fuel, pays appropriate fees, and properly maintains bulk fuel storage tanks in the AOR. (Project: TBD)	May-14	May-15	AF QA KG
COPSWA Ref. No. 1194 **Follow-Up, AFCENT War Reserved Materiel (WRM)** **Objective:** Evaluate management corrective actions taken in response to report of audit F2009-0003-FD3000, AFCENT War Reserve Materiel. Specifically, determine if AFCENT accurately identifies War Reserve Materiel requirements and authorizations, and properly accounts for War Reserve Materiel assets. (Project: TBD)	Apr-14	May-15	AF QA KG
COPSWA Ref. No. 1195 **Inter-Theater Airlift Supporting CENTCOM** Objective: Evaluate whether the Air Force effectively manages inter-theater airlift supporting CENTCOM. Specifically, determine if planners accurately plan and execute airlift configurations and load to maximize airlift capacity. (Project: TBD)	Feb-14	May-15	AF QA KW KG AE

PROJECT	START	FINAL	Country Code
COPSWA Ref. No. 1196 **Air Force Working Capital Fund Medical and Dental Inventory –** **Contractor Controlled** Objective: Determine whether key controls are effectively working to support the existence and completeness of Air Force Working Capital Fund medical/dental inventory in the AOR. Specifically, determine whether contractor personnel in the AOR properly accounted for (existence), recorded (completeness) and supported medical/dental assets. (Project: F2013-L10000-0871.000)	Jul-13	Sep-14	OM BH

Department of State Office of Inspector General

PROJECT	START	FINAL	Country Code
COPSWA Ref. No. 317 **Review of the Embassy Baghdad Air Wing Operations in Iraq (Contract Evaluation)** Objectives: Review and evaluate the procurement process to include the methods for determining the contract requirements and the contract award decisions, review the funding sources to determine allowable, allocable and reasonableness of costs claimed by the contractor, and evaluate the Department's review process for timely adjudication of invoicing and payment. (Project: 13-AUD-087)	Aug-13	Feb-14	IQ
COPSWA Ref. No. 550 **Audit of the Administration and Oversight of the Pakistan Law Enforcement Reform** Objective: Determine whether the Bureau of International Narcotics and Law Enforcement Affairs (INL) effectively managed the Pakistan Law Enforcement Reform Program. (Project: 12-AUD-049)	Oct-13	Sep-14	PK
COPSWA Ref. No. 631 **Review of Emergency Action Plan (EAP) - Embassy Islamabad (Program Evaluation)** Objective: Evaluate and assess the current status and effectiveness of the Emergency Action Plan for Embassy Islamabad to determine the reasonableness and their level of coordination and cooperation with the military commanders in-country. (Project: 13-AUD-041)	Jan-13	Sep-13	PK
COPSWA Ref. No. 995 **Audit of the Management of Department of Defense Property Transferred to the Department of State In Iraq** Objective: Determine whether the property transferred to the Department of State from the Department of Defense in Iraq is adequately accounted for, maintained, and disposed. (Project: 13-AUD-040)	Jan-13	Oct-13	IQ
COPSWA Ref. No. 997 **Audit of the Administration and Oversight of the Pakistan Counterinsurgency Capability Fund** Objective: Determine the effectiveness of the Department's administration and oversight of the programs and projects funded by the Pakistan Counterinsurgency Capability Fund. (Project: TBD)	Oct-13	Apr-14	PK

PROJECT	START	FINAL	Country Code
COPSWA Ref. No. 998 **Audit of the Award and Management of Local and Regional Contracts in Iraq** Objective: Determine whether the Department of State was following prescribed procedures when closing out local and regional contracts in Iraq. (Project: 12-AUD-84)	Dec-12	Sep-13	IQ
COPSWA Ref. No. 999 **Audit of Department of State Management of Medical Operations Supporting Personnel Assigned to Iraq** Objective: Determine whether the Department of State's management of medical operations dedicated to supporting personnel assigned to Iraq has been effective and properly resourced. (Project: TBD)	Oct-13	Mar-14	IQ
COPSWA Ref. No. 1027 **Audit of the Middle East Partnership Initiative** Objective: Determine whether the Department of State's administration and oversight of the Middle East Partnership Initiative have been effective and whether the program has achieved its stated objectives. (Project: TBD)	Oct-13	Apr-14	Multiple
COPSWA Ref. No. 1182 **Audit of the Administration of Residual Iraq Reconstruction Projects** Objective: Determine whether the Department is properly administering the completion and turnover of the residual U.S. Government-funded Iraq reconstruction projects. (Project: TBD)	Oct-13	Apr-14	IQ
COPSWA Ref. No. 1183 **Audit of the Department of State Assistance to Syrian Refugees** Objective: Determine the Department's effectiveness in managing and coordinating the humanitarian response for Syrian refugees. (Project: TBD)	Dec-13	Jun-14	SY
COPSWA Ref. No. 1184 **Audit of Construction of the New Embassy Compound - Islamabad** Objective: Determine whether the Department is effectively administering the construction contracts for the New Embassy Compound in Islamabad. (Project: TBD)	Mar-14	Sep-14	IQ
COPSWA Ref. No. 1185 **Audit of the Department of State Management of the Worldwide Protective Services Task Order for Erbil and Basrah** Objective: Determine whether the Department is effectively managing the Worldwide Protective Services Task Order for Erbil and Basrah. (Project: TBD)	Apr-14	Oct-14	IQ

PROJECT	START	FINAL	Country Code
COPSWA Ref. No. 1186 **Audit of the Conventional Weapons Destruction Program for Countries Under the Bureaus of Near Eastern Affairs and South and Central Asian Affairs** Objective: Determine whether the Bureau of Political-Military Affairs is achieving intended results through its Conventional Weapons Destruction Program. (Project: TBD)	Apr-14	Oct-14	Multiple
COPSWA Ref. No. 1187 **Audit of the Bureau of International Narcotics and Law Enforcement Affairs Counternarcotics Programs in Pakistan** Objective: Determine whether the Bureau of International Narcotics and Law Enforcement Affairs are achieving intended and sustainable results through its Counternarcotics Programs in Pakistan. (Project: TBD)	Jun-14	Dec-15	PK
COPSWA Ref. No. 1188 **Audit of the Baghdad Life Support Services Contract** Objective: Determine whether the Department is effectively managing the Baghdad Life Support Services Contract. (Project: TBD)	Sep-14	Mar-15	IQ

U.S. Agency for International Development Office of Inspector General

PROJECT	START	FINAL	Strategic Issue
COPSWA Ref. No. 770 **ACA Financial Audit on Mercy Corps** Objective: Under CAPIII for the period October 1, 2010, through September 30, 2011. (Project: 66261612)	Nov-11	Sep-13	IQ
COPSWA Ref. No. 772 **ACA Financial Audit on CHF International** Objective: Under CAPIII for the period 10/01/2010 - 09/30/2011. (Project: 66262012)	Dec-11	Sep-13	IQ
COPSWA Ref. No. 774 **ACA Financial Audit on University Research Co., LLC** Objective: Under Primary Health Care Program for the period 05/04/2011 - 03/31/2012. (Project: 66260113)	Jan-12	Sep-13	IQ
COPSWA Ref. No. 783 **DCAA Financial Audit on Bechtel National, Inc.** Objective: Under award SPU-C-00-04-00001 for the period 01/01/2005 - 01/31/2005. (Project: TBD)	Jan-11	Sep-13	IQ
COPSWA Ref. No. 784 **DCAA Financial Audit on Louis Berger Group** Objective: Under award 267-C-00-07-00500 for the period 07/01/2009 - 06/30/2010. (Project: TBD)	Jun-11	Sep-13	IQ
COPSWA Ref. No. 786 **DCAA Financial Audit on Management Systems Int'l.** Objective: Under award DFD-I-01-05-00221 for the period 10/01/2007 - 09/30/2008. (Project: TBD)	Jun-11	Sep-13	IQ
COPSWA Ref. No. 787 **DCAA Financial Audit on Louis Berger Group** Objective: Under award 267-C-00-04-00435 for the period 10/01/2007 - 03/31/2008. (Project: TBD)	Aug-11	Sep-13	IQ
COPSWA Ref. No. 788 **DCAA Financial Audit on Bechtel National, Inc.** Objective: Under award 267-CO-EEE-C-00-03-00018 for the period 01/01/2005 - 12/31/2005. (Project: TBD)	Jul-11	Sep-13	IQ

PROJECT	START	FINAL	Strategic Issue
COPSWA Ref. No. 789 **DCAA Financial Audit on Louis Berger Group** Objective: Under award 267-C-00-08-00500 for the period 01/23/2008 - 01/31/2009. (Project: TBD)	Aug-11	Sep-13	IQ
COPSWA Ref. No. 1008 **Audit of USAID/Pakistan's Small Grants and Ambassador's Fund Program** Objective: Is USAID/Pakistan's Small Grants Program achieving its goal to support the mission's development objectives that focus on development impact and address sustainability? (Project: GG101013)	Mar-13	Sep-13	PK
COPSWA Ref. No. 1009 **Audit of USAID/Pakistan's Sindh Basic Education Program** Objective: Is USAID/Pakistan's Sindh Basic Education Program achieving its goals of increasing and sustaining student enrollment in primary and secondary schools in targeted areas? (Project: GG100813)	Aug-13	Dec-13	PK
COPSWA Ref. No. 1012 **Audit of USAID/Pakistan's Government to Government Assistance Program** Objective: Is USAID/Pakistan's government to government assistance program an effective development mechanism? (Project: GG100913)	Jun-13	Oct-13	PK
COPSWA Ref. No. 1013 **Audit of USAID/Pakistan's Entrepreneurs Project** Objectives: Has USAID/Pakistan's Entrepreneurs Project succeeded in increasing incomes of 75,000 micro-entrepreneurs? Has USAID/Pakistan taken corrective action on the recommendations of Audit Report No. G-391-12-005-P? (Project: GG100613)	Aug-13	Dec 13	PK
COPSWA Ref. No. 1014 **Audit of USAID/Pakistan's Power Distribution Improvement Program** Objective: Is USAID/Pakistan's Power Distribution Improvement Program improving operational and financial performance of the eight electric power distribution companies in Pakistan by reducing losses, increasing revenues, and improving service? (Project: GG100713)	Apr-13	Oct-13	PK
COPSWA Ref. No. 1016 **Audit of USAID/Iraq's Administrative Reform Project** Objective: Has USAID/Iraq's Administrative Reform Project achieved its goal of improving the functions of its public institutions to improve service delivery processes through better governance and resource management approaches? (Project: 66152213)	Feb-13	Sep-13	IQ

PROJECT	START	FINAL	Strategic Issue
COPSWA Ref. No. 1017 **Audit of USAID/Pakistan's FATA Secretariat Capacity Building Program-Phase II** Objective: Is USAID/Pakistan's FATA Secretariat Capacity Building Program improving the capacity of governmental institutions to govern through training, automating processes, and developing management and financial systems? (Project: GG100313)	Sep-13	Jan-14	PK
COPSWA Ref. No. 1018 **Audit of USAID/Pakistan's Smallholder Dairy Project** Objective: Is USAID/Pakistan's Smallholder Dairy Project improving the skills of dairy farmers and livestock workers to increase incomes, yields, and provide improved breeding interventions? (Project: GG100413)	Oct-13	Feb-14	PK
COPSWA Ref. No. 1139 **Audit of USAID/Iraq's Elections Support Follow-on Program** Objective: Were actions taken in response to recommendations from Audit Report No. E-267-12-003-P incorporated into the follow-on program and how did they affect program performance? (Project: 66152413)	May-13	Sep-13	IQ
COPSWA Ref. No. 1269 **DCAA Financial Audit on AECOM International Development** Objective: Under award 267-C-00-10-00005 for the period 04/01/2011 - 09/30/2012. (Project: TBD)	Jun-13	Mar-14	IQ
COPSWA Ref. No. 1270 **DCAA Financial Audit on Tetra Tech DPK** Objective: Under award 267-C-00-10-00006 for the period 10/01/2011 - 03/31/2013. (Project: TBD)	Jun-13	Mar-14	IQ
COPSWA Ref. No. 1271 **DCAA Financial Audit on URC** Objective: Under award AID-267-C-11-00004 for the period 04/01/2012 - 03/31/2013. (Project: TBD)	Jun-13	Mar-14	IQ
COPSWA Ref. No. 1272 **DCAA Financial Audit on the QED Group, LLC** Objective: Under award 267-M-00-09-00513 for the period 10/01/2011 - 11/06/2012. (Project: TBD)	Jun-13	Mar-14	IQ
COPSWA Ref. No. 1273 **DCAA Financial Audit on Management Systems International** Objective: Under award AID-267-C-11-00005 for the period 04/01/2012 - 03/31/2013. (Project: TBD)	Jun-13	Mar-14	IQ

PROJECT	START	FINAL	Strategic Issue
COPSWA Ref. No. 1274 **DCAA Financial Audit on QED** Objective: Under award 267-O-00-08-00507 for the period 10/01/2011 - 09/30/2012. (Project: TBD)	Jun-13	Mar-14	IQ
COPSWA Ref. No. 1275 **DCAA Financial Audit on Louis Berger Group (LBG)** Objective: Under award 267-C-00-08-00500 for the period 01/01/2012 - 03/31/2013. (Project: TBD)	Sep-13	Jun-14	IQ
COPSWA Ref. No. 1276 **DCAA Financial Audit on Louis Berger Group (LBG)** Objective: Under award 267-C-00-07-00500 for the period 10/01/2011 - 11/30/2012. (Project: TBD)	Sep-13	Jun-14	IQ
COPSWA Ref. No. 1277 **DCAA Financial Audit on ACDI/VOCA** Objective: Under award 267-A-00-08-00504 for the period 10/01/2011 - 09/30/2012. (Project: TBD)	Sep-13	Jun-14	IQ
COPSWA Ref. No. 1278 **DCAA Financial Audit on CHF International** Objective: Under award 267-A-00-08-00503 for the period 10/01/2011 - 09/30/2012. (Project: TBD)	Sep-13	Jun-14	IQ
COPSWA Ref. No. 1279 **DCAA Financial Audit on Int'l Relief & Development** Objective: Under award 267-A-00-08-00506 for the period 10/01/2011 - 09/30/2012. (Project: TBD)	Sep-13	Jun-14	IQ
COPSWA Ref. No. 1280 **DCAA Financial Audit on Mercy Corp** Objective: Under award 267-A-00-08-00505 for the period 10/01/ 2011 - 09/30/2012. (Project: TBD)	Sep-13	Jun-14	IQ

U.S. Government Accountability Office

PROJECT	START	FINAL	Country Code
COPSWA Ref. No. 1052 **CENTCOM Posture** Objectives: GAO initiated this audit in response to a congressional mandate. This job code replaces job code 351443, which GAO had begun in response to this same mandate. Determine to what extent (1) the defense posture reflects current strategy in the region and shifted regional priorities; (2) DoD estimated and reported total future posture costs, identified cost drivers, and programmed funds; (3) DoD estimated and reported current and anticipated host nation contributions; and (4) DoD incorporates the perspective of other stakeholders when developing and implementing posture requirements. (Project: 351791)	Dec-12	Oct-13	SWA
COPSWA Ref. No. 1133 **U.S. Security Assistance to Lebanon II** Objectives: (1) To what extent has the U.S. Government funded assistance to Lebanese security services? (2) To what extent has the U.S. government implemented accountability measures, including end use monitoring, for equipment provided to Lebanese security personnel and entities? (3) To what extent does the U.S. Government vet recipients of U.S. security assistance for human rights violations? (4) How do the Lebanese security forces comply with U.S. requirements to safeguard U.S.-provided equipment? (Project: 320975)	Apr-13	Jan-14	LB
COPSWA Ref. No. 1166 **Department of State and U.S. Agency for International Development Contingency Contracting** Objectives: To what extent have State and USAID: (1) assessed their organizational structures related to contracting for overseas contingency operations and determined whether related changes are needed; (2) assessed their contract planning, management, and coordination policies for overseas contingency operations and determined whether changes to those policies are needed; and (3) assessed their acquisition workforce, including reliance on contractors, for overseas contingency operations and determined whether changes are needed? (Project: 121119)	Mar-13	Jan-14	AF IQ

Section 3. Section 852 Project

Department of Defense Office of Inspector General

Project	Start	Final	Country Code
COPSWA Ref. No. 1323 **Air Force's Performance-Based Logistics Contracts With the Lockheed Martin Corporation and the Rolls-Royce Corporation for the C-130 Hercules Aircraft** Objective: Evaluate the cost effectiveness of material purchases made for the C-130J Hercules aircraft through performance-based logistics contracts with the Lockheed Martin Corporation and the Rolls-Royce Corporation. (Project: D2013-D000CH-0157.000)	May-13	May-14	CONUS

PAGE INTENTIONALLY LEFT BLANK

Section 4. Status of Southwest Asia Projects Tracked in FY 2013, as of September 1, 2013

Section 4.0. FY 2013 Completed Projects Summary

TABLE 5. FY 2013 COMPLETED PROJECTS BY ORGANIZATION

ORGANIZATION	COMPLETED-AFGANISTAN	COMPLETED - TOTAL
DoD OIG	25	33
AAA	14	17
NAVAUDSVC	1	1
AFAA	6	8
SIGAR	41	41
SIGIR	0	9
DOS OIG	1	6
USAID OIG	19	56
GAO	15	19
Total Projects	122	190

TABLE 6. FY 2013 COMPLETED OVERSIGHT PROJECTS BY SELECT COUNTRIES

COUNTRY	Total
Afghanistan	122
Iraq	30
Kuwait	9
Pakistan	24
Qatar	9

Note: One project may affect two or more countries.

SUMMARY PRORATED OVERSIGHT COVERAGE BY FY 2013 AFGHANISTAN STRATEGIC OVERSIGHT ISSUES (as of September 1, 2013)

NUMBER OF PROJECTS BY AGENCY	DOD OIG		AAA		AFAA		NAS		SIGAR		GAO		DOS OIG		USAID OIG		Projects Per Issue (b)	
FY 2013 STRATEGIC ISSUE	Total	Closed	Total	Closed	Total	Closed	Total	Closed	Total	Closed	Total	Closed	Total	Closed	Total	Closed	Total	Closed
RECONSTRUCTION																		
1. Building the Capacity and Capabilities of the ANSF (a)	20.0	14.0							9.4	4.6	3.0	3.0					32.4	21.6
2. Administering and Maintaining Accountability of the ASFF	0.5	0.5	1.0	1.0					2.5	2.5							4.0	4.0
3. Building Afghan Governance Capacity									6.5	2.0					10.0	8.0	16.5	10.0
4. Sustaining U.S. Investment in Afghan Institutions and Infrastructure	1.0	0.5							38.0	19.5					6.0	2.0	45.0	22.0
5. Increasing Revenue Generation Within the Afghan Government									4.5	4.0							4.5	4.0
6. Implementing Civil Service and Pay Reforms Within the Afghan Government									2.5	2.0					1.0	1.0	3.5	3.0
7. Implementing Afghan Electoral Reforms and Preparing for Elections															1.0	0.0	1.0	0.0
8. Executing and Sustaining Counternarcotics Programs									2.0	2.0			1.0	0.0			3.0	2.0
9. Expanding the Capacity of and Sustaining the Afghan Justice System									5.0	2.0			2.0	1.0			7.0	3.0
10. Implementing Anti-Corruption Initiatives									1.9	1.6					1.0	0.0	2.9	1.6
11. Planning and Coordinating U.S. Assistance Programs									3.5	2.5	1.0	1.0					4.5	3.5
12. Providing Stewardship of Direct Assistance Funds									3.5	0.5					0.5	0.5	4.0	1.0
13. Awarding and Administering Reconstruction Contracts	5.5	4.0							62.9	37.6			0.5	0.0	34.5	16.5	103.4	58.1

SUMMARY PRORATED OVERSIGHT COVERAGE BY FY 2013 AFGHANISTAN STRATEGIC OVERSIGHT ISSUES (as of September 1, 2013)

NUMBER OF PROJECTS BY AGENCY	DOD OIG		AAA		AFAA		NAS		SIGAR		GAO		DOS OIG		USAID OIG		Projects Per Issue (b)	
FY 2013 STRATEGIC ISSUE	Total	Closed	Total	Closed	Total	Closed	Total	Closed	Total	Closed	Total	Closed	Total	Closed	Total	Closed	Total	Closed
OTHER THAN RECONSTRUCTION																		
14. Safety	2.5	2.5			4.0	3.0			n/a	n/a	2.0	0.0	2.0	1.0			10.5	6.5
15. Sustainment and Retrograde (a)	3.8	2.8	7.0	5.0	3.0	2.0			n/a	n/a	2.0	1.0					15.8	10.8
16. Base Closure / Transfer (a)			3.0	3.0	1.0	0.0			n/a	n/a							4.0	3.0
17. Property Management and Disposition (a)	2.0	0.0	6.0	5.0	1.0	0.0			n/a	n/a	1.0	0.0					10.0	5.0
18. Contract Management / Acquisition of Supplies and Services (a)	3.8	2.3	10.0	6.0			1.0	1.0	n/a	n/a	8.0	3.0	0.5	0.0			23.3	12.3
19. Infrastructure Management							1.0	1.0	n/a	n/a	1.0	0.0	1.0	0.0			2.0	1.0
20. Financial Management	1.0	0.5	1.0	1.0					n/a	n/a							2.0	1.5
21. Transition Planning									0.5	0.0	5.0	3.0	1.0	0.0			6.0	3.0
22. Crosscutting and Other	3.8	2.8	3.0	0.0	4.0	3.0	3.0	1.0	n/a	n/a	5.0	4.0			1.0	1.0	19.8	11.8
Total number of projects per agency (b) (c)	44	30	31	21	13	8	5	3	143	81	27	15	8	2	55	29	326	189

NOTES:
(a) Department of Defense drawdown/transition focus.
(b) A project may cover more than one issue. For example, if a project covers three strategic issues, each issue is prorated a value of 0.3. Total number of projects is rounded and represents the number of projects each agency had submitted for the FY 2013 COPSWA.
(c) Closed projects include those completed with a final report, cancelled, terminated, or no longer applicable to Southwest Asia.

Section 4.2. Southwest Asia-Related Reports Issued in FY 2013, as of September 1, 2013

Report Number	Report Title (Project Number)	Report Date	Country/ Strategic Code	COPSWA Ref. No.
DoD OIG			(http://www.dodig.mil/pubs/index.cfm)	
DODIG-2013-123	Army Needs To Improve Mi-17 Overhaul Management and Contract Administration (Project: D2012-D000AS-0075.000)	08/30/2013	CONUS PK	660
DODIG-2012-034.6 (Classified)	Assessment of Afghan National Security Forces Metrics, Afghan National Army (ANA), October 2012 – March 2013 (U) (Project: D2011-D00SPO-0182.006)	08/30/2013	AF:1	909
DODIG-2013-113	Assessment of DoD Wounded Warrior Matters – Fort Riley (Project: D2009-D00SPO-0209.004)	08/06/2013	CONUS	1019
DODIG-2013-099	Compliance With Electrical and Fire Protection Standards of U.S. Controlled and Occupied Facilities in Afghanistan (Project: D2012-DT0TAD-0001)	07/18/2013	AF:14	415
DODIG-2013-099	Compliance With Electrical and Fire Protection Standards of U.S. Controlled and Occupied Facilities in Afghanistan (Project: D2012-DT0TAD-0002)	07/18/2013	AF:14	416
DODIG-2013-100 (FOUO)	Contract Administration of the Subsistence Prime Vendor Contract for Afghanistan Improved, but Additional Actions Are Needed (Project: D2012-D000LD-0086.000)	07/02/2013	AF:15 AF:22	657
DODIG-2012.034.5 (Classified)	Assessment of Afghan National Security Forces Metrics, Ministry of Interior Police Forces, October 2012 - March 2013 (Project: D2011-D00SPO-0182.005)	06/28/2013	AF:1	810
DODIG-2013-095	Award and Administration of Radio Contracts for the Afghan National Security Forces Need Improvement (Project: D2012-D000AT-0129.000)	06/27/2013	AF:1 AF:18	669

Report Number	Report Title (Project Number)	Report Date	Country/ Strategic Code	COPSWA Ref. No.
DODIG-2013-097	Improvements Needed in the Oversight of the Medical-Support Services and Award-Fee Process Under the Camp As Sayliyah, Qatar, Base Operation Support Services Contract (Project: D2012-D000JB-0181.000)	06/26/2013	QA	897
DODIG-2013-093	DoD Needs to Improve Oversight of the Afghan National Police Training/Mentoring and Logistics Support Contract (Project: D2012-D000AS-0137.000)	06/25/2013	AF:1 AF:13	853
DODIG-2013-094	Assessment of U.S. and Coalition Efforts to Develop Leaders in the Afghan National Army (Project: D2012-D00SPO-0090)	06/24/2013	AF:1	640
DODIG-2013-087	Assessment of DoD Wounded Warrior Matters – Joint Base Lewis-McChord (Project: D2009-D00SPO-0209.007)	05/31/2013	CONUS	1022
DODIG-2013-081	Assessment of U.S. Government and Coalition Efforts to Train, Equip, and Advise the Afghan Border Police (Project: D2012-D00SPO-0210.000)	05/24/2013	AF:1	904
DODIG-2013-066 (Classified)	(U) Transportation Planning Is Sufficient for Retrograde Operations; However, There Is an Opportunity To Improve the Efficiency of Management Systems (Project: D2012-D000JA-0195.000)	04/12/2013	AF:15 AF:22	903
DODIG-2013-062	Policies and Procedures Needed to Reconcile Ministry of Defense Advisors Program Disbursements to Other DoD Agencies (Project: D2012-D000JB-0209.000)	03/28/2013	AF:1	1023
DODIG-2013-058	Assessment of U.S. Government and Coalition Efforts to Develop the Afghan National Army Command, Control, and Coordination System (Project: D2012-D00SPO-0085.000)	03/22/2013	AF:1	639
DODIG-2013-053	Oversight of U.S. Military and Coalition Efforts to Improve Healthcare Conditions and to Develop Sustainable Afghan National Security Forces Medical Logistics at the Dawood National Military Hospital (Project: D2012-D00SPO-0163.000)	03/13/2013	AF:1	857

Report Number	Report Title (Project Number)	Report Date	Country/ Strategic Code	COPSWA Ref. No.
DODIG-2013-052	Inadequate Contract Oversight of Military Construction Projects in Afghanistan Resulted in Increased Hazards to Life and Safety of Coalition Forces (Project: D2012-D000JB-0126.000)	03/08/2013	AF:13	854
DODIG-2013-050	Recovering Organizational Clothing and Individual Equipment From Civilians and Contractor Employees Remains a Challenge (Project: D2012-D000LD-0067.000)	02/22/2013	CONUS	1058 656
DODIG-2012-034.4 (Classified)	(U) Assessment of Afghan National Security Forces Metrics – Afghan National Army (ANA), March 2012 – August 2012 (Project: D2011-D00SPO-0182.004)	02/20/2013	AF:1	809
DODIG-2013-040 (FOUO)	Critical Information Needed to Determine the Cost and Availability of G222 Spare Parts (Project: D2012-D000AT-0170.000)	01/31/2013	AF:1 AF:18	667
DoDIG-2013-037	Quality Controls for the Rotary Wing Transport Contracts Performed in Afghanistan Need Improvement (Project: D2012-D000AS-0031.000)	01/15/2013	AF:15 AF:18 AF:22	666
DODIG-2013-030 (FOUO)	Counterintelligence Screening Needed to Reduce Security Threat That Unscreened Local National Linguists Pose to U.S. Forces (Project: D2010-D000JA-0165.002)	12/07/2012	AF:14 AF:18	855
DODIG-2013-026 (FOUO)	Supply Support Activities in Afghanistan Could Be Managed More Effectively to Improve Inventory Accountability (Project: D2011-D000JO-0169.000)	11/30/2012	AF:15 AF:18	458
DODIG-2013-024	U.S. Army Corps of Engineers Needs to Improve Contract Oversight of Military Construction Projects at Bagram Airfield, Afghanistan (Project: D2012-D000JB-0071.000)	11/26/2012	AF:13	365
No Report Required	Audit Research on Fixed-Wing Aircraft for the Afghan Air Force for Future Audit Projects (Project: D2012-D000AT-0171.000)	11/2012	AF:1 AF:13	866

Report Number	Report Title (Project Number)	Report Date	Country/ Strategic Code	COPSWA Ref. No.
DODIG-2013-005	Performance Framework and Better Management of Resources Needed for the Ministry of Defense Advisors Program (Project: D2012-D000JB-0093.000)	10/23/2012	AF:1	647
DODIG-2012-141 (Classified)	Assessment of U.S. Government and Coalition Efforts to Train, Equip and Field the Afghan Air Force (Project: D2011-D00SPO-0234.000)	09/28/2012	AF:1	460
DODIG-2012-034.3 (Classified)	Assessment of Afghan National Security Forces Metrics-Ministry of Interior Police Forces, Nov 2011 - Apr 2012 (Project: D2011-D00SPO-0182.000)	09/28/2012	AF:1	808
DODIG-2012-135 (FOUO)	Mi-17 Overhauls Had Significant Cost Overruns and Schedule Delays (Project: D2011-D000AS-0241.000)	09/27/2012	PK	716
DODIG-2012-138	Wholesale Accountability Procedures Need Improvement for the Redistribution Property Assistance Team Operations (Project: D2012-D000JA-0110.000)	09/26/2012	KW	849
DODIG-2012-128	Fees and Surcharges Assessed on Afghanistan Security Forces Fund Orders Need Improved Cost Accounting (Project: D2011-D000FD-0121.000)	09/19/2012	AF:2 AF:20	102
DODIG-2012-134	Contingency Contracting: A Framework for Reform 2012 Update (Project: D2012-D000CD-0141.000)	09/18/2012	CONUS	860
AAA		https://www.aaa.army.mil/default.htm) *Restricted to .mil and to GAO (.gao.gov)*		
A-2013-0117-MTE	Afghanistan Base Closure Processes (Project: A-2012-MTE-0425.000)	06/26/2013	AF:16	887
A-2013-0110-MTE (FOUO)	Acquisition Cross Servicing Agreements-Afghanistan (Project: A-2013-MTE-3711.000)	06/13/2013	AF:20	856
A-2013-0082-MTE (FOUO)	Administration of the Contractor Logistics Support Services Contract — MRAP, Afghanistan (Project: A-2012-MTE-0423.000)	04/08/2013	AF:18	886
A-2013-0067-MTE (FOUO)	Audit of Asset Visibility and Accountability During Retrograde (Project: A-2012-MTE-0422.000)	03/14/2013	AF:15	885
A-2013-0052-MTE (FOUO)	Foreign Excess Property Programs (Project: A-2012-MTE-0335.000)	03/04/2013	AF:16	859

Report Number	Report Title (Project Number)	Report Date	Country/ Strategic Code	COPSWA Ref. No.
A-2013-0056-MTE (Restricted)	Retrograde Sort Process, Afghanistan (Project: A-2012-MTE-0420.000)	02/26/2013	AF:15	883
A-2013-0054-MTE (FOUO)	Performance Metrics — National Afghan Trucking Contract, Bagram Airfield, Afghanistan (Project: A-2012-MTE-0081.000)	02/13/2013	AF:18	533
A-2013-0051-MTE	Audit of Contract Administration of the National Afghan Trucking Contract (Project: A-2012-MTE-0071.000)	02/07/2013	AF:18	527
A-2013-0048-MTE	Materiel Management — Retrograde From Southwest Asia, U.S. Army Forces Command (Project: A-2012-MTE-0073.000)	02/01/2013	AF:15	528
A-2013-0047-ALC	Accession of Military Personnel Into Contracting (Project: A-2011-ALC-0411.000)	01/31/2013	CONUS	475
A-2013-0016-MTE (Restricted)	Audit of Area Support Group-Kuwait S6 Information Technology Contracts (Project: A-2012-MTE-0262.000)	12/07/2012	KW	803
A-2013-0015-MTE	Contract Management — Atmospherics Program–Afghanistan (Project: A-2011-ALL-0490.000)	11/28/2012	AF:18	524
A-2013-0005-MTE	Army Prepositioned Stocks Southwest Asia (Project: A-2011-ALL-0094.000)	11/07/2012	KW QA	49
A 2012 0204-ГMГ (Restricted)	Direct Contributions From Afghanistan Security Forces Fund (Project: A-2012-FMF-0345.000)	09/28/2012	AF:2	881
A-2012-0146-MTE	Bulk Fuel Accountability in Afghanistan-Phase II (Project: A-2011-ALL-0330.000)	09/27/2012	AF:17	436
A-2012-0186-MTE	Financial Transparency in the Afghan Transportation Network-South Contract, Bagram Airfield, Afghanistan (Project: A-2011-ALL-0534.000)	09/21/2012	AF:18	526
A-2012-0184-MTE (FOUO)	Audit of Found on Installation Property (Project: A-2012-MTE-0240.000)	09/20/2012	AF:17	802
NAVAUDSVC	**(Phone: 202-433-5757 or DSN 288-5757)**			
IGMC Control 10612	Afghanistan Contracting Assessment (Project: 2013-010)	04/16/2013	AF:18	1043

Report Number	Report Title (Project Number)	Report Date	Country/ Strategic Code	COPSWA Ref. No.
AFAA			(http://www.afaa.af.mil)	
F2013-0010-O30000	Follow-up Audit, United States Forces Central Deployed Locations Aerial Port Operations (Project: F2012-O30000-0493)	08/26/2013	AF:22 KW KG QA AE	804
F2013-0009-O30000	Personnel Deployment and Redeployment (Project: F2012-O30000-0491)	06/26/2013	AF:14 KW KG QA	514
F2013-0008-L40000	Shipment of Controlled Items From the United States Air Forces Central Area of Responsibility (Project: F2012-L40000-0033)	06/10/2013	AF:14 KW QA	515
F2013-0002-L20000	United States Air Forces Central Area of Responsibility Base-Level Inventory (Project: F2012-L20000-0227)	02/26/2013	AF:22	54
F2013-0003-O30000	Follow-Up Audit: Pre-Positioned Mobility Bags (Project: F2011-O30000-0460)	02/08/2013	KW KG QA	66
F2013-0002-L40000	Mine Resistant Ambush Protected Vehicles (Project: F2011-L40000-0033)	01/29/2013	AF:22 KW QA	65
F2013-0002-L30000	United States Air Forces Central Area of Responsibility (Project: F2011-L30000-0007)	01/23/2013	KW KG QA AE	52
F-2013-0002-O40000	Medical Aspects of Contractor Deployments (Project: F2012-O40000-0114)	11/26/2012	AF:14 KG QA AE	512
SIGAR			(http://www.sigar.mil)	
SIGAR Audit 13-15	Afghanistan Public Protection Force: Concerns Remain About Force's Capabilities and Costs (Project: SIGAR-074A)	07/30/2013	AF:1	1040
SIGAR Audit 13-16	Stability in Key Areas (SIKA) Programs: After 16 Months and $47 Million Spent, USAID Had Not Met Essential Program Objectives (Project: SIGAR-076A)	07/29/2013	AF:4	1060

Report Number	Report Title (Project Number)	Report Date	Country/ Strategic Code	COPSWA Ref. No.
SIGAR Financial Audit 13-11	Department of State's Afghanistan Media Project: Audit of Incurred Costs by HUDA Development Organization Afghanistan (Project: SIGAR-F-011)	07/26/2013	AF:13	949
SIGAR Inspection 13-10	Bathkhak School: Unauthorized Contract Design Changes and Poor Construction Could Compromise Structural Integrity (Project: SIGAR-I-005D)	07/24/2013	AF:4 AF:13	1088
SIGAR Audit 13-14	Contracting With the Enemy: State and USAID Need Stronger Authority to Terminate Contracts When Enemy Affiliations Are Identified (Project: SIGAR 66-A)	07/24/2013	AF:13	1305
SIGAR Special Project 13-8	Improvised Explosive Devices: Unclear Whether Culvert Denial Systems to Protect Troops Are Functioning or Were Ever Installed (Project: SIGAR-SP-3)	07/23/2013	AF:9	1051
SIGAR Inspection 13-9	Sheberghan Teacher Training Facility: U.S. Army Corps of Engineers Paid Contractors and Released Them From Contractual Obligations Before Construction Was Completed and Without Resolving Serious Health and Safety Hazards (Project: SIGAR-I-006D)	07/17/2013	AF:4 AF:13	1096
SIGAR Inspections 13-8	Forward Operating Base Salerno: Inadequate Planning Resulted in $5 Million Spent for Unused Incinerators and the Continued Use of Potentially Hazardous Open-Air Burn Pit Operations (Project: SIGAR I-007)	07/16/2013	AF:4	1039
SIGAR Financial Audit 13-10	USAID's Alternative Livelihoods Program–Eastern Region: Audit of Costs Incurred by Development Alternatives, Inc. (Project: SIGAR-F-003)	07/18/2013	AF:13	940
SIGAR Financial Audit 13-9	USAID's Alternative Development Project South/West: Audit of Costs Incurred by Tetra Tech AR (Project: SIGAR-F-007)	07/18/2013	AF:13	943

Report Number	Report Title (Project Number)	Report Date	Country/ Strategic Code	COPSWA Ref. No.
SIGAR Financial Audit 13-7	Department of Defense Program to Support the Afghan National Army's Technical Equipment Maintenance Program: Audit of Costs Incurred by Afghan Integrated Support Services (Project: SIGAR-F-001)	07/17/2013	AF:13	948
SIGAR Financial Audit 13-8	Department of Defense Program to Support the Afghan National Army's Technical Equipment Maintenance Program: Audit of Costs Incurred by Afghan Integrated Support Services (Project: SIGAR-F-005)	07/16/2013	AF:13	941
SIGAR Alert 13-4	Alert Letter: Camp Leatherneck Incinerators, Burn Pit Being Used (Project: SIGAR-I-007G)	07/11/2013	AF:4	1121
SIGAR Audit 13-12	Department of State's Assistance Awards: Afghanistan Reconstruction Activities Are Largely Unaudited (Project: SIGAR-065A)	07/08/2013	AF:13	890
SIGAR Financial Audit 13-6	Financial Audit of USDA Cooperative Agreement 58-3148-1-042 With Volunteers for Economic Growth Alliance (VEGA) for the Capacity Building and Change Management Program for the Ministry of Agriculture, Irrigation, and Livestock (Project: SIGAR-F-010)	07/03/2013	AF:13	947
SIGAR Audit 13-13	Afghan Special Mission Wing: DoD Moving Forward With $771.8 Million Purchase of Aircraft that the Afghans Cannot Operate and Maintain (Project: SIGAR-064A)	06/28/2013	AF:8 AF:13	891
SIGAR Alert 13-2	Southern Regional Agriculture Development Program Had Poor Coordination, Waste, and Mismanagement (Project: SIGAR-058A)	06/27/2013	AF:13	893
SIGAR Financial Audit 13-5	USAID's Program to Support the Loya Jirga and Election Process in Afghanistan: Audit of Costs Incurred by The Asia Foundation (Project: SIGAR-F-004)	06/27/2013	AF:13	946
SIGAR SP-13-4	Management Alert Letter: Subcontractors Nonpayment Issues (Project: SIGAR-SP-5)	06/17/2013	AF:13	1306

Report Number	Report Title (Project Number)	Report Date	Country/ Strategic Code	COPSWA Ref. No.
SIGAR Financial Audit 13-4	USAID's Technical Support to the Central and Provincial Ministry of Public Health Project: Audit of Costs Incurred by Management Sciences for Health (Project: SIGAR-F-006)	06/13/2013	AF:13	942
SIGAR Financial Audit 13-3	Audit of Costs Incurred by Futures Group International, LLC in Support of USAID's Project for Expanding Access to Private Sector Health Products and Services in Afghanistan (Project: SIGAR-F-009)	06/06/2013	AF:13	945
SIGAR Financial Audit 13-2	Audit of Costs Incurred by Cardno Emerging Markets Group, LTD. In Support of USAID's Afghanistan State-Owned Enterprises Privatization, Excess Land Privatization, and Land Titling Project (Project: SIGAR-F-008)	06/06/2013	AF:13	944
SIGAR Financial Audit 13-1	Audit of Costs Incurred by Chemonics International, Inc. in Support of USAID's Alternative Livelihoods Program-Southern Region (Project: SIGAR-F-002)	06/06/2013	AF:13	939
SIGAR Audit 13-8	Taxes: Afghan Government Has Levied Nearly a Billion Dollars in Business Taxes on Contractors Supporting U.S. Government Efforts in Afghanistan (Project: SIGAR-060A)	05/14/2013	AF:5	821
SIGAR Audit 13-9	Health Services in Afghanistan: Two New USAID Funded Hospitals May Not Be Sustainable and Existing Hospitals Are Facing Shortages in Some Key Medical Positions (Project: SIGAR-068A)	04/29/2013	AF:4	1313
SIGAR Inspection 13-7	Qala-I-Muslim Medical Clinic: Serving the Community Well, but Construction Quality Could Not Be Fully Assessed (Project SIGAR-I-005G)	04/17/2013	AF:4 AF:13	938
SIGAR Inspection 13-6	Afghan National Police Main Road Security Company, Kunduz Province, Is Behind Schedule and May Not Be Sustainable (Project: SIGAR-I-006I)	04/17/2013	AF:4 AF:13	683

Report Number	Report Title (Project Number)	Report Date	Country/ Strategic Code	COPSWA Ref. No.
SIGAR Audit 13-6	Contracting With The Enemy: DoD Has Limited Assurance That Contractors With Links To Enemy Groups Are Identified And Their Contracts Terminated (Project: SIGAR-066A)	04/11/2013	AF:13	936
SIGAR Audit 13-7	Afghanistan's National Power Utility: Commercialization Efforts Challenged by Expiring Subsidy and Poor USFOR-A and USAID Project Management (Project: SIGAR-063A)	04/2013	AF:5	899
SIGAR SP 13-3	Management Safety Alert Letter (K-Span ANA Facilities) (Project: SIGAR-SP-9)	04/04/2013	AF:13	1154
SIGAR SP-13-2	Afghan National Security Forces: Limited Visibility Over Fuel Imports Increases The Risk That U.S.-Funded Fuel Purchases Could Violate U.S Economic Sanctions Against Iran (Project: SIGAR-SP-2)	01/30/2013	AF:2 AF:12	1053
SIGAR Inspection 13-5	Imam Sahib Border Police Company Headquarters In Kunduz Province: $7.3 Million Facility Sits Largely Unused (Project: SIGAR-I-006C)	01/29/2013	AF:2	1307
SIGAR Inspection 13-4	Kunduz Afghan National Police Provincial Headquarters: After Construction Delays And Cost Increases, Concerns Remain About the Facility's Usability And Sustainability (Project: SIGAR-I-006)	01/24/2013	AF:2	1308
SIGAR Audit 13-4	Afghan National Army: Controls Over Fuel for Vehicles, Generators, and Power Plants Need Strengthening to Prevent Fraud, Waste, and Abuse (Project: SIGAR-054A)	01/24/2013	AF:1 AF:10 AF:13	675
SIGAR Audit 13-3	Afghan Police Vehicle Maintenance Contract: Actions Needed to Prevent Millions of Dollars From Being Wasted (Project: SIGAR-052A)	01/17/2013	AF:1 AF:13	673
SIGAR Audit 13-2	Afghanistan's National Power Utility: $12.8 Million in DoD-Purchased Equipment Sits Unused, and USAID Paid a Contractor for Work Not Done (Project: SIGAR-063A)	12/18/2012	AF:5	684

Report Number	Report Title (Project Number)	Report Date	Country/ Strategic Code	COPSWA Ref. No.
SIGAR SP-13-1	Anti-Corruption Measures: Persistent Problems Exist in Monitoring Bulk Cash Flows at Kabul International Airport (Project: SIGAR-067A)	12/11/2012	AF:10	935
SIGAR Audit 13-1	Afghan National Security Forces Facilities: Concerns With Funding, Oversight, and Sustainability for Operation and Maintenance (Project: SIGAR-049A)	10/30/2012	AF:1 AF:13	232
SIGAR Inspection 13-3	Gamberi Afghan National Army Garrison: Site Grading and Infrastructure Maintenance Problems Put Facilities at Risk (Project: SIGAR-I-002)	10/30/2012	AF:4 AF:13	682
SIGAR Inspection 13-2	Wardak Province National Police Training Center: Contract Requirements Generally Met, but Deficiencies and Maintenance Issues Need to Be Addressed (Project: SIGAR-I-004)	10/30/2012	AF:4 AF:13	702
SIGAR Inspection 13-1	Kunduz ANA Garrison: Army Corps of Engineers Released DynCorp of All Contractual Obligations Despite Poor Performance and Structural Failures (Project: SIGAR-I-001)	10/25/2012	AF:4 AF:13	681
SIGAR (Not Tracked in COPSWA)			**(http://www.sigar.mil)**	
SIGAR Alert 13-6	Serious Deficiencies Related to the Afghanistan Justice Training Transition Program Administered by the Department of State	07/22/2013	N/A	None
SIGAR SP-13-7	Management Alert: Command and Control Facility at Camp Leatherneck	07/08/2013	N/A	None
SIGAR Alert 13-5	Concerns With Chemonics International, Inc. Meeting Its Responsibilities Under Federal Contract	07/02/2013	N/A	None
SIGAR Alert 13-3	Afghan Government Levying Additional Fines, Fees, and Penalties That May Cost U.S. Government Millions of Dollars	06/28/2013	N/A	None
SIGAR SP-13-6	Safety Alert Letter (Sheberghan Teacher Training Facility)	06/21/2013	N/A	None
SIGAR SP-13-5	Safety Alert Letter (Bathkhak School)	06/21/2013	N/A	None
SIGAR Alert-13-1	National Geospatial-Intelligence Agency Analysis on Afghanistan Infrastructure and Security Cartography System	01/29/2013	N/A	None

Report Number	Report Title (Project Number)	Report Date	Country/ Strategic Code	COPSWA Ref. No.
SIGAR Alert	Destruction of Operation Enduring Freedom Financial Documents Related to Afghan National Army Petroleum, Oil, and Lubricants (SIGAR-054A)	09/10/2012	N/A	675
SIGIR				(http://www.sigir.mil)
N/A	Learning From Iraq: A Final Report From the Special Inspector General for Iraq Reconstruction culminates SIGIR's nine-year mission overseeing Iraq's reconstruction. It serves as a follow-up to SIGIR's previous comprehensive review of the rebuilding effort, Hard Lessons: The Iraq Reconstruction Experience.	03/2013	IQ	1073
SIGIR 13-006	Government Agencies Cannot Fully Identify Projects Financed With Iraq Relief and Reconstruction Funds (Project: 1205)	03/06/2013	IQ	858
Special Report Number 3	Special Report Number 3: Interagency Rebuilding Efforts in Iraq: A Case Study of the Rusafa Political District (Project: LL1101)	02/26/2013	IQ	800
SIGIR 13-005	Lessons Learned on the Department of Defense's Commander's Emergency Response Program in Iraq (Project: 1302)	01/24/2013	IQ	994
SIGIR 13-004	Lessons Learned From U.S. Agencies' Management of Iraqi Funds for Relief and Reconstruction (Project: 1301)	01/22/2013	IQ	993
SIGIR 13-001	Sustaining the Progress Achieved by U.S. Rule of Law Programs in Iraq Remains Questionable (Project: 1020)	11/25/2012	IQ	481
N/A	Iraq Reconstruction: Lessons from Auditing U.S.-Funded Stabilization and Reconstruction Activities (Project: 1206)	10/2012	IQ	871
SIGIR 13-003	Development Fund for Iraq: U.S. Army Corps of Engineers Has Missing Receiving Reports and Open Task Orders (Project: 1112d)	10/26/2012	IQ	894

Report Number	Report Title (Project Number)	Report Date	Country/ Strategic Code	COPSWA Ref. No.
SIGIR 13-002	Final Review of the State Department's Management of Quick Response Funds in 2007 and 2008 (Project: 1203b)	10/26/2012	IQ	992
DOS OIG	(http://oig.state.gov/lbry/index.htm)			
AUD-MERO-13-33	Audit of the U.S. Mission Iraq Staffing Process (Project: 12-AUD-077)	08/13/2013	IQ	540
AUD-MERO-13-25	Audit of Bureau of Diplomatic Security Worldwide Protective Services Contract – Task Order 5 for Baghdad Movement Security (Project: 12-AUD-50)	03/27/2013	IQ	541
AUD-MERO-13-20 (SBU)	Evaluation of Emergency Action Plans for U.S. Mission Afghanistan (Project: 11-MERO-1875)	03/21/2013	AF:14	628
AUD-MERO-13-18	"Restricted Report Title" (Project: 11-MERO-3014)	12/31/2012	PK	313
AUD-MERO-12-46 (SBU)	Evaluation of the Local Guard Force Contract for Embassy Islamabad and Consulates General Karachi, Lahore, and Peshawar (Project: 11-MERO-3015)	09/27/2012	PK	314
AUD-MERO-12-47 (SBU)	Compliance Followup Review of Department of State Actions to Reduce the Risk of Trafficking in Persons Violations in Four States in the Cooperation Council for the Arab States of the Gulf (Project: 12-AUD-012)	09/24/2012	OTHER	733
USAID OIG	(http://oig.usaid.gov/auditandspecialbyyear/USAID)			
F-306-13-002-S	Audit of USAID/Afghanistan's Use of Third-Country National Employees (Project: FF101412)	08/31/2013	AF:22	607
F-306-13-015-N	Closeout Audit of the Fund Accountability Statement of USAID Resources Managed by the Islamic Republic of Afghanistan Through the Ministry of Transport and Civil Aviation Under the Regional Airports Project, Implementation Letter No. 306MlLMIIM05-17 for the Period From January 9, 20 II to July 31 , 2012 (Project: FF200912)	8/31/2013	AF:13	591

Report Number	Report Title (Project Number)	Report Date	Country/ Strategic Code	COPSWA Ref. No.
F-306-13-014-N	Audit of the Costs Incurred in Afghanistan by Chemonics International Under The Regional Afghan Municipalities Program for Urban Populations (RAMPUP) in RC-South, Contract No. 306-C-00-10-00527-00, for the Period June 10, 2010, to December 31, 2011 (Project: FF200113)	07/30/2013	AF:13	848
F-306-13-013-N	Close-out Audit of USAID Resources Managed by Creative Associates International Inc. Under the Ambassador's Small Grants Program, Cooperative Agreement No. 306-A-00-09-00517-00 for the Period July 2, 2009, to January 31, 2012 (Project: FF200312)	07/24/2013	AF:13	740
F-306-13-012-N	Closeout Audit of USAID Resources Managed by Ministry of Communications and Information Technology to Implement Policy Capacity Initiative Activity, Implementation Letter No. 306-IL-09-12-0004.00 for the Period From October 1, 2010, to March 31, 2011 (Project: FF200812)	06/27/2013	AF:3	1045
F-306-13-011-N	Financial Audit of Costs Incurred in Afghanistan Under the USAID Contract No. 306-1-00-06-00517 With the Joint Venture Louis Berger Group, Inc./Black & Veatch Special Projects Corp. for the Period October 01, 2010, to September 30, 2011 (Project: FF200112)	06/26/2013	AF:13	1044
6-267-13-008-D	Independent Audit of Management System International, Inc., Costs Incurred and Billed Under USAID Contract No. DFD-I-00-05-00221, for the Period From October 1, 2008, to July 31, 2011 (Project: 6690B213)	06/26/2013	IQ	744

Report Number	Report Title (Project Number)	Report Date	Country/ Strategic Code	COPSWA Ref. No.
6-267-13-007-D	Independent Audit of Garda World Consulting Inc., Subaward No. 267-A-00-04-00405-00, Under International Foundation for Election Systems/Consortium for Election and Political Process Strengthening, Agreement No. DGC-A-00-01-00004-00, for the Period From July 1, 2007, to September 30, 2011 (Project: 6690B313)	06/26/2013	IQ	1281
G-391-13-025-R	Financial Audit of the Program Titled: "Gender Equity Program," USAID/Pakistan Agreement No. 391-A-00-10-01162-00, Managed by Aurat Publication and Information Service Foundation, for the Year Ended June 30, 2012 (Project: GG902513)	06/18/2013	PK	1282
6-267-13-006-D	Independent Audit of International Foundation for Election Systems, IFES, Inc., Consortium for Election and Political Process Strengthening, Costs Incurred and Billed Under Cooperative Agreement No. 267-A-00-04-00405-00, From July 1, 2009, to February 29, 2012 (Project: 6690B013)	06/16/2013	IQ	749
6-267-13-005-D	Independent Audit of AECOM International Development, Inc., Costs Incurred and Billed Under USAID Contract No. 267-I-021-06-0015, for the Period From October 1, 2010, to January 6, 2012 (Project: 6690B113)	06/16/2013	IQ	751
6-267-13-013-P	Audit of USAID/Iraq's Primary Health Care Project in Iraq (Project: 66151713)	06/16/2013	IQ	1011
6-267-13-002-S	Survey of Security Services Employed by USAID/Iraq's Contractors and Grantees (Project:EE100212)	06/13/2013	IQ	621

Report Number	Report Title (Project Number)	Report Date	Country/ Strategic Code	COPSWA Ref. No.
F-306-13-010-N	Audit of the Costs Incurred in Afghanistan by Chemonics International Inc. Under the Trade Accession and Facilitation for Afghanistan Project, Contract No. 306-C-00-09-00S29-00 for the Period From November 18, 2009, Through November 15, 2012 (Project: FF200513)	06/13/2013	AF:13	584
G-391-13-004-P	Audit of USAID/Pakistan's Agribusiness Project (Project: GG100513)	06/12/2013	PK	1010
6-267-13-031-N	Audit of the Fund Accountability Statement of USAID Resources Managed by International Relief and Development Under Cooperative Agreement No. 267-A-00-08-00506, Community Action Program (ICAPIII), for the Period From October 1, 2010, to September 30, 2011 (Project: 66261912)	05/30/2013	IQ	771
6-267-13-030-N	Audit of the Fund Accountability Statement of USAID Resources Managed by International Relief and Development Under Cooperative Agreement No. 267-A-00-08-00506, Community Action Program (ICAPIII), for the Period From October 1, 2008, to September 30, 2010 (Project: 66261112)	05/30/2013	IQ	795
F-306-13-009-N	Audit of Costs Incurred in Afghanistan by The Asia Foundation (TAF) Under the Afghan Public Opinion Surveys Program, Cooperative Agreement No. 306-A-00-09-00514-00 for the Period June 23, 2009, to September 30, 2011 (Project: FF200512)	05/29/2013	AF:13	835

Report Number	Report Title (Project Number)	Report Date	Country/ Strategic Code	COPSWA Ref. No.
G-391-13-024-R	Financial Audit of the Project Titled "Monitoring and Evaluation Project," USAID/Pakistan Contract No. 391-C-00-10-01138-00, and Program Titled "Assessment and Strengthening Program," USAID/Pakistan Cooperative Agreement No. 391-A-00-11-01203-00, Managed by Associates in Development (Private) Limited, for the Year Ended June 30, 2012 (Project: GG902413)	05/29/2013	PK	1153
F-306-13-008-N	Closeout Audit of the USAID Resources Managed by Aga Khan Trust for Culture Under Urban Revitalization Program, Grant Agreement No. 306-G-00-10-00529-00 From June 23, 2010, to October 31, 2011 (Project: FF201112)	05/23/2013	AF:13	588
G-391-13-023-R	Financial Audit of the Program Titled: "USAID's Citizens' Voice Project," USAID/Pakistan Contract No. AID-391-C-11-00001, Managed by Trust for Democratic Education and Accountability, for the Period May 27, 2011, to June 30, 2012 (Project: GG902313)	05/23/2013	PK	1152
G-391-13-003-P	Audit of USAID/Pakistan's Independent Monitoring and Evaluation Program (Project: GG100912)	05/22/2013	PK	617
G-391-13-022-R	Financial Audit of the USAID Resources Managed by National Rural Support Programme, for the Year Ended June 30, 2012 (Project: GG902213)	05/20/2013	PK	1151
G-391-13-001-N	Financial Audit of the Program Titled: "Accelerated Capacity Building of Provincial Reconstruction, Rehabilitation and Settlement Authority/Provincial Disaster Management Authority," USAID/Pakistan Contract No. 391-C-00-10-01144-00, Managed by KPMG Taseer Hadi & Co., for the Period February 16, 2010, to January 31, 2012 (Project: GG200513)	05/17/2013	PK	1150

Report Number	Report Title (Project Number)	Report Date	Country/ Strategic Code	COPSWA Ref. No.
6-267-13-029-N	Audit of Fund Accountability Statement of Local Costs Incurred, Under Cooperative Agreement No. 267-A-00-08-00504-00, Managed by Agricultural Cooperative Development International/Volunteers in Overseas Cooperative Assistance, Community Action Program III, for the Period From October 1, 2010, to September 30, 2011 (Project: 66261212)	05/15/2013	IQ	794
G-391-13-021-R	Financial Audit of the Program Titled: "USAID Agribusiness Project," USAID/Pakistan Agreement No. AID-391-A-12-00001, Managed by Agribusiness Support Fund, for the Period From November 10, 2011, to June 30, 2012 (Project: GG902113)	05/15/2013	PK	1148
G-391-13-004-O	Report on Financial Review Procedures Performed on USAID Resources (Local Cost), Managed by the Education Development Center Inc., USAID Agreement No. 391-A-11-00001, Program Titled: "Pre-Service Teacher Education," for the Period April 5, 2011, to December 31, 2011 (Project: GG200413)	05/15/2013	PK	1149
F-306-13-007-N	Financial Audit of Costs Incurred in Afghanistan by Roots of Peace Under the Commercial Horticulture and Agriculture Marketing Program, Cooperative Agreement No. 306-A-00-10-00512 for the Period From February 1, 2010, to December 31, 2011 (Project: FF201212)	05/14/2013	AF:13	836
6-267-13-028-N	Close-out Audit of the Cost Representation Statement of USAID Resources Managed by Development Alternative Inc., Contract No. 267-C-00-07-00505-00, Iraq Rapid Assistance Program, for the Period From October 1, 2009, to September 30, 2010 (Project: 66261012)	04/30/2013	IQ	796
G-391-13-001-S	Review of USAID/Pakistan's International Training Practices (Project: GG101113)	04/30/2013	PK	1140

Report Number	Report Title (Project Number)	Report Date	Country/ Strategic Code	COPSWA Ref. No.
F-306-13-006-N	Financial Audit of USAID Resources, Managed by the Government of the Islamic Republic of Afghanistan Through the Ministry of Finance, Under the Civilian Technical Assistance Program, Grant Agreement No. 306-09-CTAP-0001 for the Period From October 01, 2010, to March 20, 2012 (Project: FF201012)	04/30/2013	AF:6	1046
6-267-13-027-N	Audit of the Cost Representation Statement of Locally Incurred Costs of USAID Resources Managed by Management Systems International, Under Contract No. AID-267-C-11-00005, Iraq Administrative Reform Project-Tarabot, for the Period From June 5, 2011, to March 31, 2012 (Project: 66261712)	04/29/2013	IQ	776
G-391-13-020-R	Financial Audit of Projects Managed by Lahore University of Management Sciences: Foreign Recipient Contracted Assessment and Strengthening Program Under Cooperative Agreement No. 391-A-00-11-01202-00, and Sub Recipient Contracted Merit and Needs Based Scholarship Program Under Grant Agreement No. 391-G-00-04-01023-00, for the Year Ended June 30, 2012 (Project: GG902013)	04/15/2013	PK	1147
G-391-13-003-O	Report on Financial Review Procedures Performed on USAID Resources (Local Cost) Managed by the American Institute of Research, USAID Agreement No. 391-A-00-08-01100-00, Program Titled: "Links to Learning: Education Support to Pakistan Program," for the Period From July 1, 2010, to December 31, 2011 (Project: GG200313)	04/05/2013	PK	1146
G-391-13-019-R	Financial Audit of USAID/Pakistan Grant Agreement No. 391-IL-00-08-01111-00, Managed by Health Services Academy (HSA), for the Period From July 1, 2011, to June 30, 2012 (Project: GG901913)	04/04/2013	PK	1145

Report Number	Report Title (Project Number)	Report Date	Country/ Strategic Code	COPSWA Ref. No.
G-391-13-018-R	Financial Audit of the Program Titled "Anti-Corruption Program Pakistan," USAID/Pakistan Cooperative Agreement No. 391-A-00-09-01117-00, for the Project Ended December 31, 2011, and Program Titled "Anti-Fraud Hotline," USAID/Pakistan Cooperative Agreement No. 391-A-00-10-01194-00, Managed by Transparency International Pakistan, for the Year Ended June 30, 2012 (Project: GG901813)	04/01/2013	PK	1144
G-391-13-002-P	Audit of USAID/Pakistan's Gender Equity (Project: GG100213)	03/28/2013	PK	1006
G-391-13-001-Q	Quality Control Review of the Audit Report and Audit Documentation for the Financial Audit Conducted by Horwath Hussain Chaudhury & Co. of USAID/Pakistan Cooperative Agreement No. 391-A-00-11-01206-00, Managed by Dairy Rural Development Foundation, for the Year Ended June 30, 2012 (Project: GG930113)	03/08/2013	PK	1143
F-306-13-005-N	Financial Audit of Costs Incurred in Afghanistan by the Citizen Network for Foreign Affairs Under the Afghanistan Farm Services Alliance Program, Cooperative Agreement No. 306-A-00-08-00517-00 for the Period January 1, 2010, to September 30, 2011 (Project: FF200212)	03/17/2013	AF:13	834
G-391-13-017-R	Financial Audit of USAID/Pakistan Cooperative Agreement No. 391-A-00-11-01206-00, Managed by Dairy Rural Development Foundation (DRDF), for the Year Ended June 30, 2012 (Project: GG901713)	03/08/2013	PK	1142
F-306-13-004-N	Financial Audit of Local Costs Incurred by Deloitte Consulting LLP Under "The Economic Growth & Governance Initiative," USAID Contract No. 306-EEM-I-04-07-00005 for the Period August 15, 2009, to September 30, 2010 (Project: FF200412)	02/28/2013	AF:13	569

Report Number	Report Title (Project Number)	Report Date	Country/ Strategic Code	COPSWA Ref. No.
G-391-13-016-R	Financial Audit USAID/Pakistan Grant Agreement No. 391-IL-08-01111-00, Managed by Health Service Academy (HSA), for the Period From July 1, 2009, to June 30, 2010 (Project: GG901613)	02/22/2013	PK	1141
6-267-13-015-N	Audit of Fund Accountability Statement of Local Costs Incurred, Under Cooperative Agreement No. 267-A-00-08-00504-00, Managed by Agricultural Cooperative Development International/Volunteers in Overseas Cooperative Assistance (ACDI/VOCA), Community Action Program III, for the Period From October 1, 2008, to September 30, 2010 (Project: 66261312)	02/12/2013	IQ	773
G-391-13-001-P	Audit of USAID/Pakistan's Design for Sustainability in the Design of the Jamshoro Thermal Power Station Repair and Rehabilitation Project (Project: GG100212)	01/17/2013	PK	610
F-306-13-003-N	Closeout Audit of USAID Resources, Managed By the International Organization for Migration Under the Afghan Civilian Assistance Program, Cooperative Agreement No. 306-A-00-07-00516-00 for the Period From June 5, 2007, to November 30, 2011 (Project: FF200612)	01/10/2013	AF:13	571
6-267-13-004-D	Independent Audit of Incurred and Billed Costs USAID Purchase Order 267-O-00-08-00507-00 (Manpower) September 13, 2008, Through September 30, 2011, the QED Group, LLC (Project: 66900313)	12/19/2012	IQ	767
6-267-13-003-D	Independent Audit of Incurred and Billed Costs USAID Delivery Order 267-O-00-09-00513-00 (Perform) September 30, 2009, through September 30, 2011, the QED Group, LLC (Project: 66900213)	12/19/2012	IQ	768
6-267-13-004-P	Audit of USAID/Iraq's Access to Justice Program (Project: EE100412)	12/16/2012	IQ	622

Report Number	Report Title (Project Number)	Report Date	Country/ Strategic Code	COPSWA Ref. No.
F-306-13-002-N	Close-out Audit of Local Costs Incurred and Billed by Oasis International Schools, Inc. Under the "Establishment of International School of Kabul," Cooperative Agreement No. 306-A-00-05- 00522-00 for the Period From May 27, 2005, to December 31, 2010 (Project: FF201011)	11/29/2012	AF:13	565
F-306-13-001-N	Financial Audit of American University of Afghanistan (AUAF), Support for the American University of Afghanistan (AUAF) (Project: FF200911)	10/24/2012	AF:13	741
F-306-13-001-S	USAID/Afghanistan's Performance Based Governors' Fund (Project: FF100312)	10/12/2012	AF:3	596
6-267-13-001-P	Audit of USAID/IRAQ'S Legislative Strengthening Program (Project: EE100112)	10/03/2012	IQ	620
F-306-13-001-R	Financial Audit of the Program "Regenerating Murad Khane, Restoring Refurbishing and Revitalizing the Old City," Cooperative Agreement No. 306-A-09-00503-00, Managed by the Turquoise Mountain Trust (TMT), for the Period From January 1, 2011, to December 31, 2011 (Project: FFFF900412)	10/03/2012	AF:13	589
G-391-12-009-P	Audit of USAID/Pakistan's Assessment and Strengthening Program (Project: GG100412)	09/30/2012	PK	612
F-306-12-002-S	Review of USAID/Afghanistan's Monitoring and Evaluation System (Project: FF101812)	09/26/2012	AF:12 AF:13	847
6-267-12-044-N	Audit of the Cost Representation Statement of Locally Incurred Costs by AECOM, Under Contract No. 267-C-00-10-00005-00, Iraq Financial Development Project-IFDP, for the Period From July 18, 2010, to September 30, 2011 (Project: 66261812)	09/12/2012	IQ	775

Report Number	Report Title (Project Number)	Report Date	Country/ Strategic Code	COPSWA Ref. No.
GAO			(http://www.gao.gov)	
Classified	Issued Classified Report (Project: 351772)	08/02/2013	AF:21	1037
Classified	Issued Classified Report (Project: 351742)	06/28/2013	Multiple	880
Classified	Classified Report (Project: 351747)	06/2013	AF:1	898
GAO-13-427	Pakistan Reporting on Visa Delays That Disrupt U.S. Assistance Could Be Improved (Project: 320938)	05/07/2013	PK	1028
GAO-13-381	Security Force Assistance More Detailed Planning and Improved Access to Information Needed to Guide Efforts of Advisor Teams in Afghanistan (Project: 351743)	04/30/2013	AF:1	873
GAO-13-426SU	Military Information Support Operations: Improved Coordination, Evaluations, and Training and Equipping Are Needed (Project: 351733)	04/26/2013	AF:22	1031
GAO-13-319R	DoD Procurement of Mi-17 Helicopters (Project:121096)	04/01/2013	AF:21	1050
GAO-13-196	International Religious Freedom Act State Department and Commission Are Implementing Responsibilities but Need to Improve Interaction (Project: 320901)	03/26/2013	AF:22	1030
GAO-13-310	U.S. Assistance to Yemen Actions Needed to Improve Oversight of Emergency Food Aid and Assess Security Assistance (Project: 320921)	03/20/2013	YE	900
GAO-13-289	Security Assistance Evaluations Needed to Determine Effectiveness of U.S. Aid to Lebanon's Security Forces (Project: 320918)	03/19/2013	LB	1134
GAO-13-251R	Defense Contracting: Actions Needed to Explore Additional Opportunities to Gain Efficiencies in Acquiring Foreign Language Support (Project: 351726)	02/25/2013	AF:18	879
GAO-13-218SP	Afghanistan: Key Oversight Issues (Project: 320924)	02/11/2013	AF:22	988

Report Number	Report Title (Project Number)	Report Date	Country/ Strategic Code	COPSWA Ref. No.
GAO-13-212	Warfighter Support: DoD Needs Additional Steps to Fully Integrate Operational Contracts Support into Contingency Planning (Project: 351692)	02/08/2013	AF:18 IQ	870
GAO-13-182	Military Personnel: DoD Has Taken Steps to Meet the Health Needs of Deployed Servicewomen, but Actions Are Needed to Enhance Care for Sexual Assault Victims (Project: 351718)	01/29/2013	AF:22	865
GAO-13-185R	Afghanistan Drawdown Preparations: DoD Decision Makers Need Additional Analyses to Determine Costs and Benefits of Returning Excess Equipment (Project: 351688)	12/19/2012	AF:15	814
GAO-13-34	Afghanistan Development: Agencies Could Benefit from a Shared and More Comprehensive Database on U.S. Efforts (Project: 320889)	11/07/2012	AF:11	815
GAO-12-977R	Iraq and Afghanistan: Agencies Are Taking Steps to Improve Data on Contracting but Need to Standardize Reporting (Project: 121049)	09/21/2012	AF:18 IQ	852
Brief (FOUO)	Issued Oral Briefing (Project: 320940)	09/13/2012	AF: 1	1029
Classified	Issued Classified Report (Project: 320856)	09/11/2012	AF:21	722

Appendix A. Scope and Methodology

The Department of Defense Office of Inspector General, Office of the Deputy Inspector General for Southwest Asia (DIG-SWA) prepared this FY 2014 Comprehensive Oversight Plan for Southwest Asia (COPSWA). The COPSWA includes descriptions of oversight projects—audits, inspections, and evaluations—of activities that directly affect efforts in Southwest Asia and surrounding areas. This FY 2014 COPSWA identifies a total of 315 Southwest Asia related oversight projects: 185 ongoing and 130 planned for FY 2014, as of September 1, 2013.

Project information on the ongoing and planned oversight efforts contained in this plan was submitted by the following Southwest Asia Joint Planning Group (SWA JPG) contributing organizations:

- Department of Defense Office of Inspector General
- U.S. Army Audit Agency
- Naval Audit Service
- U.S. Air Force Audit Agency
- Special Inspector General for Afghanistan Reconstruction
- Department of State Office of Inspector General
- U.S. Agency for International Development Office of Inspector General, and
- U.S. Government Accountability Office.

The information for the plan was obtained directly from the contributing organizations, which also validated the content submitted for accuracy and completeness. All decisions regarding the selection, location, and dates of projects were made by the respective contributing organization. DIG-SWA staff compiled the report and reviewed the content for potential duplicative planned projects, errors, omissions, and timing updates. Where unclear input was identified, the DIG-SWA staff asked the respective organization to review and clarify the highlighted attributes of each questioned project. As a result of these discussions, an agency may have decided to withdraw, cancel, or terminate a project, or provide additional information that clarified the objectives, focus, or dates of a project.

After the consolidated draft COPSWA was prepared, it was distributed to each contributing organization for an opportunity to validate the content of the plan and to make final adjustments or updates to the plan, as necessary. During this phase, each organization also reviewed the consolidated draft COPSWA to identify, coordinate, and resolve any further potential duplication issues directly with other contributing organization(s).

At the end of this review and validation process, all final changes were submitted and made, and the final COPSWA was prepared and issued.

For FY 2014, the COPSWA includes an updated Joint Strategic Oversight Plan for Afghanistan. This FY 2014 joint plan was developed by SWA JPG contributing organizations with emphasis on Afghanistan because most of the ongoing and planned oversight work in Southwest Asia is occurring in Afghanistan or is related to Afghanistan. See Section 1.0 of the FY 2014 COPSWA for the complete FY 2014 Joint Strategic Oversight Plan for Afghanistan, which is presented in two sections: 1. Reconstruction and 2. Other Than Reconstruction.

Because of the significance of ongoing U.S. missions in Afghanistan, during FY 2012, the SWA JPG established two subgroups to develop a Joint Strategic Oversight Plan for Afghanistan to include in the COPSWA. These subgroups agreed to meet each year to update the plan. The subgroup chaired by the Special Inspector General for Afghanistan Reconstruction, led an effort to update the plan for Afghanistan Reconstruction issues. The subgroup chaired by the Department of Defense Office of Inspector General, led an effort to update the plan for Other Than Reconstruction issues in Afghanistan. The joint plan was also coordinated with the remaining SWA JPG contributing organizations.

A comparison of the FY 2013 joint plan with the FY 2014 joint plan shows that the 13 strategic oversight issues previously identified for Reconstruction and the 9 issues for Other Than Reconstruction (22 total) in FY 2013 were consolidated to 7 Reconstruction and 4 Other Than Reconstruction strategic oversight issues (11 total) in FY 2014, as converted below:

Table A.1. Comparison of Issues for the Joint Strategic Oversight Plan for Afghanistan	
FY 2013	**FY 2014**
Section 1. Reconstruction	
1. Building the Capacity and Capabilities of the Afghanistan National Security Forces 2. Administering and Maintaining Accountability of the Afghanistan Security Forces Fund	1. Building the Capacity and Capabilities of the Afghan National Security Forces and Administering and Maintaining Accountability of the Afghanistan Security Forces Fund
3. Building Afghan Governance Capacity 6. Implementing Civil Service and Pay Reforms Within the Afghan Government 7. Implementing Afghan Electoral Reforms and Preparing for Elections	2. Building Afghan Governance Capacity
4. Sustaining U.S. Investment in Afghan Institutions and Infrastructure 5. Increasing Revenue Generation Within the Afghan Government	3. Sustaining U.S. Investment in Afghan Institutions and Infrastructure
8. Executing and Sustaining Counternarcotics Programs	4. Executing and Sustaining Counternarcotics Programs
9. Expanding the Capacity of and Sustaining the Afghan Justice System 10. Implementing Anti-Corruption Initiatives	5. Implementing Anti-Corruption Initiatives
11. Planning and Coordinating U.S. Assistance Programs 12. Providing Stewardship of Direct Assistance Funds	6. Planning, Coordinating, and Providing Stewardship of Direct and Indirect Assistance Funds and Programs
13. Awarding and Administering Reconstruction Contracts	7. Awarding and Administering Reconstruction Contracts

Table A.1. Comparison of Issues for the Joint Strategic Oversight Plan for Afghanistan	
FY 2013	**FY 2014**
Section 2. Other Than Reconstruction	
14. Safety	8. Health and Safety
15. Sustainment and Retrograde 17. Property Management and Disposition	9. Retrograde and Property Management
18. Contract Management/Acquisition of Supplies and Services 20. Financial Management	10. Contract Management and Oversight
16. Base Closure/Transfer 19. Infrastructure Management 21. Transition Planning	11. Transition Planning and Execution
22. Crosscutting and Other	N/A

Specific oversight projects that address the 11 Afghanistan strategic oversight issues and associated focus areas are identified in Section 1 of the FY 2014 COPSWA. The FY 2014 Afghanistan project summary matrix in Section 1.1 is based on the individual projects listed in Sections 1.2 and 1.3. Each strategic oversight issue is numbered as a code, as identified in Table 1. Projects with more than one strategic oversight issue code are counted on a prorated basis for the summary.

Projects previously included in the FY 2013 COPSWA that were either ongoing or planned as of September 1, 2013, were carried over in the FY 2014 COPSWA, and are included in Sections 1 and 2, respectively, along with new projects proposed for FY 2014. For Sections 1 and 2 of the COPSWA, projects are listed by the executing SWA JPG organization; and in the order of the unique COPSWA reference number. A reference number is assigned by the DIG-SWA staff for each project submitted by a SWA JPG contributing organization, and is a unique identifier for tracking purposes only. Section 2 of the FY 2014 COPSWA identifies oversight projects for Southwest Asia countries other than Afghanistan. See Table 2 for country codes.

Section 3 is included in the COPSWA for reporting purposes and is in response to the reporting requirements contained in Public Law 110-417, "The National Defense Authorization Act for Fiscal Year 2009," section 852, "Comprehensive Audit of Spare Parts, Purchases, and Depot Overhaul and Maintenance of Equipment For Operations in Iraq and Afghanistan," October 14, 2008. See Appendix B for legislative mandates that relate to the COPSWA.

Section 4 of the FY 2014 COPSWA provides information on oversight project activity during FY 2013, as of September 1, 2013. Section 4.0 summaries completed projects by agency and country. The FY 2013 Afghanistan project summary matrix at Section 4.1 provides the total number of projects and those closed (completed, terminated, or cancelled) during FY 2013, based on the FY 2013 Afghanistan strategic codes. Section 4.2 lists final and special-purpose reports issued during FY 2013, grouped by the respective SWA JPG agency.

Some products are listed in Section 4.2 that do not contain a COPSWA reference number because the oversight work was not submitted in advance for inclusion in the COPSWA tracking, such as for quick response memorandum, and special alert reports and letters. When these products are also released to the public, they are included in the COPSWA product listing as the result of additional oversight conducted in Southwest Asia.

In March 2013, the Special Inspector General for Iraq Reconstruction (SIGIR) culminated its nine-year mission in the issuance of its study, "Learning From Iraq: A Final Report From the Special Inspector General for Iraq Reconstruction." As such, SIGIR did not submit carryover or new oversight projects for the FY 2014 COPSWA. Final reports that SIGIR issued during FY 2013 are listed in Section 4.2.

The Southwest Asia countries identified in Sections 2, 3, and 4 of the FY 2014 COPSWA are within the U.S. Central Command's area of responsibility, and are alphabetically coded as follows:

Table A.2. Southwest Asia Country Codes
(U.S. Central Command's Area of Responsibility)

AF	Afghanistan	OM	Oman
BH	Bahrain	PK	Pakistan
EG	Egypt	QA	Qatar
IR	Iran, Islamic Republic of	SA	Saudi Arabia
IQ	Iraq	SY	Syrian Arab Republic
JO	Jordan	TJ	Tajikistan
KZ	Kazakhstan	TM	Turkmenistan
KW	Kuwait	AE	United Arab Emirates
KG	Kyrgyzstan	UZ	Uzbekistan
LB	Lebanon	YE	Yemen
Southwest Asia issue with work conducted elsewhere:			
CONUS = Continental United States OCONUS = Outside the Continental U.S.		Other/Multiple = Not exclusively a Southwest Asia country.	

Source: International Organization for Standardization, ISO 3166-1-Alpha-2 Country Codes.

Appendix B. Legislative Mandates

Section 842

Public Law 110-181, "The National Defense Authorization Act for Fiscal Year 2008," section 842, "Investigation of Waste, Fraud, and Abuse in Wartime Contracts and Contracting Processes in Iraq and Afghanistan," January 28, 2008, requires the Inspector General of the Department of Defense to develop a comprehensive plan for a series of audits of Department of Defense contracts, subcontracts, and task and delivery orders for the logistical support of coalition forces in Iraq and Afghanistan. The Act also requires that the Special Inspectors General for Iraq Reconstruction and Afghanistan Reconstruction develop a comprehensive plan for a series of audits of Federal agency contracts, subcontracts, and task and delivery orders for the performance of security and reconstruction functions in Iraq and Afghanistan.

Section 852

This FY 2012 COPSWA update also includes the Department of Defense Office of Inspector General, Army Audit Agency, Naval Audit Service, and Air Force Audit Agency planned and ongoing oversight efforts related to Public Law 110-417, "The National Defense Authorization Act for Fiscal Year 2009," section 852, "Comprehensive Audit of Spare Parts, Purchases, and Depot Overhaul and Maintenance of Equipment For Operations in Iraq and Afghanistan," October 14, 2008, which states:

> COMPREHENSIVE AUDIT OF SPARE PARTS PURCHASES AND DEPOT OVERHAUL AND MAINTENANCE OF EQUIPMENT FOR OPERATIONS IN IRAQ AND AFGHANISTAN.
>
> (a) AUDITS REQUIRED.-The Army Audit Agency, the Navy Audit Service, and the Air Force Audit Agency shall each conduct thorough audits to identify potential waste, fraud, and abuse in the performance of the following:
>
> (1) Department of Defense contracts, subcontracts, and task and delivery orders for-
>
> (A) depot overhaul and maintenance of equipment for the military in Iraq and Afghanistan; and
>
> (B) spare parts for military equipment used in Iraq and Afghanistan; and
>
> (2) Department of Defense in-house overhaul and maintenance of military equipment used in Iraq and Afghanistan.
>
> (b) COMPREHENSIVE AUDIT PLAN.-
> (1) PLANS.-The Army Audit Agency, the Navy Audit Service, and the Air Force Audit Agency shall, in coordination with the Inspector General of the Department of Defense, develop a comprehensive plan for a series of audits to discharge the requirements of subsection (a).

(2) INCORPORATION INTO REQUIRED AUDIT PLAN.- The plan developed under paragraph (1) shall be submitted to the Inspector General of the Department of Defense for incorporation into the audit plan required by section 842(b)(1) of the National Defense Authorization Act for Fiscal Year 2008 (Public Law 110-181; 122 Stat. 234; 10 U.S.C. 2302 note).

(c) INDEPENDENT CONDUCT OF AUDIT FUNCTIONS.-All audit functions performed under this section, including audit planning and coordination, shall be performed in an independent manner.

(d) AVAILABILITY OF RESULTS.-All audit reports resulting from audits under this section shall be made available to the Commission on Wartime Contracting in Iraq and Afghanistan established pursuant to section 841 of the National Defense Authorization Act for Fiscal Year 2008 (122 Stat.230).

(e) CONSTRUCTION.-Nothing in this section shall be construed to require any agency of the Federal Government to duplicate audit work that an agency of the Federal Government has already performed.

Acronyms

AAA	Army Audit Agency
ACA	Agency Contracted Audits
AFAA	Air Force Audit Agency
AFCENT	U.S. Air Forces Central Command
AFEMS	Air Force Equipment Management Systems
ANA	Afghan National Army
ANP	Afghan National Police
ANSF	Afghan National Security Forces
AOR	Area of Responsibility
ASFF	Afghanistan Security Forces Fund
CENTCOM	U.S. Central Command
CDP	Community Development Program
CONUS	Continental United States
COPSWA	Comprehensive Oversight Plan for Southwest Asia
CSTC-A	Combined Security Transition Command-Afghanistan
DCAA	Defense Contract Audit Agency
DIG-SWA	Deputy Inspector General for Southwest Asia
DoD OIG	Department of Defense Office of Inspector General
DOS OIG	Department of State Office of Inspector General
FY	Fiscal Year
GAO	U.S. Government Accountability Office
GIRoA	Government of the Islamic Republic of Afghanistan
INL	DOS Bureau of International Narcotics and Law Enforcement
ISAF	International Security Assistance Force
LOGCAP	Logistics Civil Augmentation Program
MoD	Ministry of Defense
NATO	North Atlantic Treaty Organization
NAVAUDSVC	Naval Audit Service

OCONUS	Outside the Continental United States
RCA	Recipient Contracted Audits
SIGAR	Special Inspector General for Afghanistan Reconstruction
SIGIR	Special Inspector General for Iraq Reconstruction
SWA	Southwest Asia
TBD	To Be Determined
USACE	U.S. Army Corps of Engineers
USAID OIG	U.S. Agency for International Development Office of Inspector General
USFOR-A	U.S. Forces-Afghanistan

www.ingramcontent.com/pod-product-compliance
Lightning Source LLC
Chambersburg PA
CBHW081325310526
45789CB00018B/2367